T0129169

MY *Bowie* STORY

MY *Bowie* STORY

Memories of David Bowie

DALE K. PERRY

MY BOWIE STORY
MEMORIES OF DAVID BOWIE

iUniverse books may be ordered through booksellers or by contacting:

iUniverse
1663 Liberty Drive
Bloomington, IN 47403
www.iuniverse.com
1-800-Authors (1-800-288-4677)

ISBN: 978-1-5320-3011-6 (sc)
ISBN: 978-1-5320-3010-9 (e)

Library of Congress Control Number: 2017913393

Print information available on the last page.

iUniverse rev. date: 09/20/2017

For Karyn
My friend in Florida

CONTENTS

Preface xi

Acknowledgements xv

Illustration Credits.. xvii

Introduction xix

Beginnings

My Most Treasured Bowie Possession by Kevin White 1

In Memory of a Free Festival by Patti Brett 3

The Birth of a Bowie Fan by Paul Kinder 5

The Man Who Thrilled the World by Sheva Golkow 9

The Gig that Changed My Life by Stuart Dalzell....................... 11

The Glitter Years by Jackie Miles... 17

The Story of Sigma Sound & the Sigma Kids by Patti Brett......21

And My Life Was Changed

A Rainy Afternoon in Philadelphia by Mark W. Falzini 27

Bowie Dropped Into My Life by Barbara Streun 31

How David Bowie Taught Us to Welcome Our Next
Days by Daniel F. Le Ray... 35

Bowie and I by Julie Stoller 37

A Reality Tour by Kathryn Kopple 41

If I Had a Time Machine by Alyssa Linn Palmer 45

From Labyrinth To Lazarus by Melanie Krichel 47

A Place In My Life by Lisa Taylor 49

Friendship and Love by Princess Ramsey 53

Perhaps I Could... by Isabelle Flows...........................55

Radio Gaga by RaMoana 57

Nothing Much at Stake by Peter Jackson.........................59

Berlin Was Where We Should Have Been by Charlie Raven 63

Makeup and Feather Boas and Sequins by Christina Prass 69

I Found Bowie, Then I Found Me by Caroline Thompson........73

It Happened One Day

Your Car is Outside by Patti Brett..............................77

Eavesdropping on Bowie by Chris Hughes 79

Bowie Slept in My Bed by Chris Buxbaum.........................81

Waiting for David —— Leipzig 1997 by Simone Metge 85

I Was Supposed to See Hilda Ogden...but saw David
Bowie Instead by Tracey Chorlton 87

The Autograph is in the Mail by Marla Kanevsky 91

Bowie Myths by Anonymous.......................................93

We All Sang in Unison by Bella Aptekar.........................99

I Wrote to Bowie and Bowie Wrote Back by Eric Isaacson.....101

A Premier and a Hello by Steve Lock...........................103

Dublin 1999 by Simone Metge 105

What Shall I Wear? by Billy Nevins 107

My Bonkers Welsh Friend by Wendy Norman.......................109

Bowie, Aldo Bagli and I by Patrizia Pezzola 111

David Has Just Left His Hotel by Mike Gately..................113

Close Encounter with a Superman by RaMoana 115

Moments in Time

Memories submitted by Sandra Atkins, Ray Nash, Patti Brett, Alyson Lewis, Randy Marthins, Jean Marie Dawson, Johnny Quest, RaMoana, Dorothy Kulisek, Michele Krichel, Gwenn Catterfeld, Debbie Pagel, Dave Wisniewski, Mark W. Falzini, Dale K. Perry and Bob Wigo

Through The Decades

The Year of the Diamond Dogs and More by Patti Brett.........155

There's a Star Man by Linda A. Metz 159

And There Won't Be Any Trouble by Frank Moriarty 163

Bowie and a Choc-Ice by Stuart Dalzell 169

My Fantastic Voyage by Denise Heptinstall 175

My Date with Bowie by Jasmine Storm 179

Serious Moonlight, Wonderful Memories by Ruth Davison ...183

Five Years by Petter M. Ness 185

Waiting for the Man by John Davey 189

A Tour of the Stadium by Patti Brett..........................195

Those Flying Machines by Dale K. Perry 197

Do You Remember Me? by Marla Kanevsky 201

"For Simone..." by Simone Metge 203

Absolute Chatters by RaMoana 205

The Birthday Concert – A Tale of Two Guests by Kali
and Belle 207

The Night David Bowie Swore at Me! by Sam 217

If Only There Was Something Between Us...Other than
our Avatars by RaMoana 219

The Reunion by Patti Brett 221

Don't Thank Me, Thank David by Sandra (Spidey) Atkins 223

I Gotta Message for The Action Man by RaMoana................233

Raining Like Crazy — NYC 2006 by Simone Metge 239

The World is Different Now
(And We are All Changed)

Bowie: Rock of Ages by Will Putney 245

Rainbows in January by Jenn Staib 247

Moon Blue by Theresa Bradley................................251

Why David Bowie is Important to Me by Patti Brett.............255

Changing the World by Sandra (Spidey) Atkins 257

The Relic by Patrick Bamburak 261
The Fantastic Voyage (1997–2013–2016–20??) by Anonymous. 263
A Beautiful Exit by Dara O'Kearney 271
Contributors 281

Reader Resources 285

PREFACE

*T*HERE ARE MOMENTS IN time that your soul — your essence — retains as a memory that never goes far from consciousness. It may not be until decades have passed that you look back and realize the strength of that memory and impact that moment had on your life.

I co-purchased my first Bowie album when I was twelve. My friend Karyn and I walked to the shopping center and while I suspect she knew we were looking for a David Bowie album, I didn't know that. Karyn always was so aware of the important things in the world and, if nothing else, was a voracious reader of the Sunday Philadelphia newspapers and listener of Philadelphia radio stations. And so, there we were. I can still picture us in the store, holding the record album and putting our money together as we went to purchase the album that had that "Space Oddity" song.

I wasn't sure I actually liked the music. But I loved the lyrics and the voice and that was enough, for then. As time went by, discovering David Bowie was performing in Philadelphia (a half hour away from our home) was pure torture; he might well have been at the North Pole, there was no hope in going to a concert as we were too young to drive. A few years later, although still too young to drive but old enough to be daring, I went to my first Bowie concert. It was at the Spectrum and last minute tickets had gone on sale. I came up with the $7.50 for the ticket, told my parents I was staying at a friend's house, and convinced a guy known as "Tin Grin" to drive us to Philadelphia. We arrived only to find that our seats were behind the stage. It didn't matter. I was in the same building as David Bowie; I could hear him and see the back of him. All was fine.

Somewhere over time, Bowie became a subconscious fixture in my life that seemed as natural as knowing I needed air to breathe. I think of all the important times of my life — good and bad — and, still today, if I shut my eyes and listen closely I will hear the Bowie music that accompanies the event. What happened to me is no different than what thousands of other fans worldwide have experienced. Perhaps naively, I didn't realize that many people who knew me or worked with me were aware of the impact Bowie had on my life. Sadly, in January 2016, I found out how obvious it had been to others that there was a special place within my being that functioned by the mere existence of David Bowie. I received texts, emails, calls and cards all with the same message: this is very strange and we don't quite know what to say, but we know the death of Bowie will be so difficult for you. It's hard to understand mourning someone who you didn't know and who never knew you.

Which brings me to this book, *My Bowie Story*. In the months after Bowie's death and after the celebrity tributes disappeared, the most touching stories I read would be those from his fans. The pieces were little moments in time that were unexpected, unrehearsed and genuine. I would want to go back and reread some of those stories, but I could never locate them again. They had disappeared into cyberspace, especially if I didn't know where they were originally posted. I knew I wanted these Bowie stories in a book — a genuine, old fashioned book that I could hold in my hands and read over and over again. With no connection to the official Bowie world, I took a leap of faith and decided to see if anyone would send me their story to be put into a book. The response from the Bowie contingent was slow at first, but then it all came together — it is *their* Bowie story.

The sound of David Bowie's voice has always inspired and calmed me at the same time. It helps me focus and puts me in a place of limitless optimism. That is how *My Bowie Story* came to be. In my heart, the Bowie legacy is the inspiration to go further, to be more than you think you can be and most of all, to be true to yourself.

Dale K. Perry
West Trenton, NJ
June 2017

ACKNOWLEDGEMENTS

$\mathcal{T}$HE SIMPLE PHRASE "THANK YOU" does not seem sufficient to express my gratitude to the people who participated in the creation of *My Bowie Story*. I hope they realize that I am forever grateful for ensuring this book became a reality.

Mark W. Falzini has served in many varied capacities in the making of *My Bowie Story*. Initially I asked Mark to perform a "little" research that turned into him becoming a sounding board, technical advisor and advocate for the project. Later, he was given the job of proofreader and copyeditor. Make no mistake, were it not for Mark there would be *zero* photographs in this book. Many thanks to Mark aka "the graphic(s) guy!"

A special thank you also goes to Wayne McDaniel, proofreader, copyeditor and overall supporter who answered a variety of questions without any hesitation. I don't even know if he likes David Bowie, but he sure seemed to like the book.

Sandra (Spidey) Atkins was one of the first people I ran the project idea past. She's been on board since the beginning and is the most positive, inspiring person on this planet! Thank you Spidey!

A huge thank you goes to the amazing Patti Brett. She launched the initial project notice during dinner one evening in August 2016 and has been a resource and advocate for *My Bowie Story* ever since. Patti's kindness and enthusiasm are unmatched.

Special thanks to Dagmar for her photographs and generosity.

The effervescent and always energetic RaMoana also provided notice of the project via her radio show, offered great ideas on getting the information to the Bowie world and has been a major supporter during the entire process.

Paul Kinder generously posted the project notice on his website, *Bowie Wonderworld*, which provided a way to reach Bowie fans worldwide. Much appreciated!

I also thank each and every person who submitted their story. I know that some writers were hesitant about sharing their personal feelings and I especially thank them for showing how their lives were permanently changed by Bowie. I also thank those who were aware of the project, didn't have a story to submit but continuously wrote to give their encouragement. It was greatly appreciated.

Finally, and most of all, thank you David.

ILLUSTRATION CREDITS

Cover – Patti Brett, Mike Garson, David Bowie, Larry Washington, Tony Visconti — Sigma Sound Studios, Philadelphia PA, 1974 – *Photo by Dagmar*

Sketch – "Bowie" by *Artemis Burns*

1. The "penny" with permission from *Kevin White*.
2. Sigma Sound Studios, Philadelphia, PA 1974 – *Photo by Dagmar*
3. Philadelphia Mural Art with permission from *Stephen Powers*
4. Philadelphia Mural Art with permission from *Stephen Powers*
5. Philadelphia Mural Art with permission from *Stephen Powers*
6. Philadelphia Mural Art with permission from *Stephen Powers*
7. Bowie Room with permission from *Julie Stoller*
8. Potsdam 2003 with permission from *Barbara Streun*
9. Ticket 1979 with permission from *Steve Lock*
10. Dublin 1999 with permission from *Simone Metge*
11. Manchester, 1997, with permission from *Mike Gately*
12. Manchester, 1997, with permission from *Mike Gately*
13. The Chili Pepper, Ft. Lauderdale, FL 1997 with permission from *RaMoana*

14. The Chili Pepper, Ft. Lauderdale, FL 1997 with permission from *RaMoana*
15. The Chili Pepper, Ft. Lauderdale, FL 1997 with permission from *RaMoana*
16. Ticket, 1997 with permission from *RaMoana*
17. The Hammersmith Apollo, 2002, with permission from *Sandra Atkins*
18. Frankfurt, Germany, 2003 with permission from *RaMoana*
19. Berlin, Germany, 2016 with permission from *Melanie Krichel*
20. Washington, DC, 1997, with permission from *Gwenn Catterfeld*
21. Washington, DC 1997, with permission from *Gwenn Catterfeld*
22. Bowie Fans with permission from *Debbie Pagel*
23. Poster with permission from *Jasmine Storm*
24. Karon Bihari Poster with permission from *Frank Moriarty*
25. Philadelphia, PA, 1997, with permission from *Marla Kanevsky*
26. Autographed shirt (1) with permission from *Simone Metge*
27. Autographed shirt (2) with permission from *Simone Metge*
28. Doobies, Philadelphia, PA, 1995 with permission from *Patti Brett*
29. Reunion 1995 with permission from *Marla Kanevsky*
30. Bowie Tattoo with permission from *Matteo Moyer*
31. Bowie Chair with permission from *Theresa Bradley*
32. HMV, 2002 with permission from *Sandra Atkins*
33. NYC, 2016, at the Cutting Room Bowie Tribute with permission from *Patti Brett*
34. Blackstar/Sigma Tattoo with permission from *Noah Webster*
35. NYC, Lazarus Premier, December 7, 2015 with permission from *Barbara Streun*

Author Photo courtesy of Erica Haller Photography, Hamilton, NJ

INTRODUCTION

ON THE PROCESS OF arranging *My Bowie Story*, I have discovered that just about everyone I encounter has some little Bowie story. My surgeon's favorite song is "Rebel, Rebel," a neighbor's daughter used to sing "Changes" while strapped in her car seat and I had a boss who frequently tried to convince us what a great job we had by belting out "Golden Years" on a daily basis.

My Bowie Story spans over four decades of memories written by Bowie fans located in eight different countries. The storytellers are a variety of ages, have different backgrounds, an assortment of occupations and the majority are not writers. Yet they all had a Bowie story to share.

Reading this book is like entering a time machine. The stories will make you laugh or cry or maybe both. In some instances they will take you back in time to what seems like a different world. One recurring theme is that David Bowie, whether through his music or his personas, provided the freedom for his fans to be whoever they needed to be in life. That message of take a risk and don't worry about what anyone else may think runs throughout *My Bowie Story*. It is incredibly inspiring.

The goal in putting together this book was to retain the voice of the individual writer. Read each story slowly and travel along to become a part of the excitement, panic or sheer joy the storyteller was feeling. I ask that you read with a gentle heart, understanding that time and distance may alter some memories. The underlying premise, however, will remain true: that the event described was one of monumental importance to the writer and remains a highlight of their life.

It is my hope that you enjoy reading *My Bowie Story* as much as I have enjoyed putting it together.

All proceeds will be donated to charity
in memory of David Bowie.

"In London there are rock cliques – very much as jazz had its cliques." [said Bowie].

And at the moment, of course, the major preoccupation of these cliques is trying to determine a successor to the throne abdicated last year by the Beatles. But David Bowie is staying out of that.

"Someone will come along," he said. "It may take a year or two, but it will happen. Right now everyone is having a go at it, and we'll just have to wait and see who comes out on top."

Jack Lloyd
The Philadelphia Inquirer
February 28, 1971

I can't understand why all the world doesn't love David Bowie. He is currently into all the right things and doing them as well as anyone around, yet sales figures prove all the world doesn't love Bowie. There seems to be only a few of us.

Which doesn't mean Bowie isn't good — just unnoticed so far. Once he is noticed, we're confident all the world will love him.

Jim Knippenberg
The Cincinnati Enquirer
January 8, 1972

BEGINNINGS

MY MOST TREASURED
BOWIE POSSESSION

Kevin White, UK

I WAS BORN AT MY parent's house on Foxgrove Avenue, Bromley in 1958. There were a lot of kids in the area, and we often got into mischief as kids will. Many times there was a knock at our door from a fed up neighbor about how the kids were running wild. We weren't, of course — well, not by today's standards anyway. One day my mother suggested that we should join the Scouts. She thought it would keep us out of trouble and that "we might learn something useful." So about six of us went along to join the 18th Bromley Scout pack in 1969. It was a great time and I made some good friends, two of whom I still have regular contact with today. It made all the difference to my life and I think in all honesty saved me from myself. Looking back, I just might have been at a crossroads and the Scouts were just what I needed.

Every year we used to do this activity called Bob-A-Job week. The idea was to raise funds by helping locals with little jobs such as gardening, sweeping leaves, shopping for the elderly and so on. I was given Foxgrove Avenue as that's where I still lived at the time. The problem was that I'd annoyed quite a few of the neighbours which resulted in most of them shutting the door on me or simply not answering the bell. Well, maybe I deserved it.

I walked up Foxgrove Avenue and knocked on a few doors but I was having no luck. I was really fed up. I began trudging back up the road when I saw a couple carrying shopping from a car. I seized the moment and asked the man if I could wash his car. He said "it's not my car, but you know I think that's a good idea." The man took my pail and sponge that my dad had loaned me and moments later the lady returned it brimming with foaming bubbles. I did the best I could. Thinking back, it wasn't how you really wash a car but I did my best. When I finished I knocked at their door and the man gave me a penny. It was the first penny I'd actually earned. I had pocket money before, but this was my first taste of employment. I kept the penny as in those days I collected all sorts of things like books of matches, postcards, toy cars and all those things kids collected.

It was sometime later, when Space Oddity had become a hit, my dad was showing me something in the local paper and I recognized the man. I told my dad, "I washed his car." My Dad said, "That's David Bowie and if he ever gets famous you will have a story to tell."

I became a Bowie fan in my teens like millions of other kids. I realized years later that the lady that brought me the pail with bubbles was Mary Finnegan. I'm not sure if the car was a Riley; I seem to recall it was a regular four-door, like an Austin Cambridge type style.

I tell people that my first employer was David Bowie and they laugh when I say that I washed his car. I have kept that penny and I still have it, even though we went to the decimal in the 1970s. I've had the penny in my pocket since the day David died. It's my most treasured item. It reminds me of a great childhood and happy times – things were so much more gentle back then. The fact that David said something positive to me when everyone else had turned me down said so much about the man.

IN MEMORY OF A FREE FESTIVAL

Patti Brett, USA

On the fall of 1972 I was driving home from school with some friends when a song came on the radio. One of my friends said, "Roll the windows up! It's David Bowie, don't let any of the sound out." I was puzzled but complied. The song was "Memory of a Free Festival." That day sealed my fate.

About a month later I found out David Bowie was going to be playing three nights in December at the Tower Theater. I wasn't allowed to take off from school to get tickets when they went on sale, but a friend got me a ticket for the Saturday night show. The shows were completely sold out, so there was no chance of getting tickets for one of the other shows.

A few weeks before the show, we learned that Mott the Hoople was scheduled to play the Tower Theater on November 30th. This was the day before the Bowie shows. I liked Mott and was excited to go see them, but best of all it was announced that David Bowie would be introducing them.

The Mott show quickly approached and on the day of the show I was so elated I could hardly contain myself. The show began and David walked out on the stage and introduced Mott. I don't really remember any of the show until David came on the stage again and sang "All the Young Dudes." The memories are a little foggy, but I had seen David in person!

I wasn't at the Tower the next night for the Bowie show as I didn't have tickets, but then Saturday finally arrived. I got to my seat and could hardly believe I was about to see my new found idol. The lights dimmed and the Walter Carlos version of Beethoven's "Ode to Joy" began to play. The lights went up to the sound of "Hang On To Yourself" as the show began. There David was — on the stage and looking so incredible my jaw dropped. It stayed that way the rest of the show (when I wasn't singing along). I knew my life had changed that night and I would never be the same. I can't explain what happened, but the combination of Mick Ronson's soaring guitar, Trevor Bolder's tight bass lines and Woody Woodmansey keeping time on the drums – all with seeing this magical creature named David — affected me to my core. I never had seen anything like David Bowie before, but I knew I wanted to see more.

Since I didn't have tickets for the last show the next night, I decided I just *had* to be at the theater. I wasn't able to get in, but I could hear the show through the thick walls. Disappointed, I still went home on cloud nine. I couldn't wait to see him again. My wait wouldn't be long — seven more shows were added in February of 1973. By then, I was completely obsessed. This obsession has taken me through 44 years of great stories, great music and a deep love for David Bowie.

THE BIRTH OF A BOWIE FAN

Paul Kinder, UK

1972

*W*E WENT ON HOLIDAY to Cornwall did Mum and me. A song came on the car radio and it totally blew me away. I later found out that the hazy cosmic jive was called "Starman" by someone called "Bowie." Then I saw him on TV, on *Top of the Pops*. I thought he was an alien. Everybody thought he was an alien. He was an alien. I was eleven. I was besotted.

I bought it next day with my holiday spends. All I need now is a record player! Can't wait to get back home. I'm sick of looking at an orange label. "I wonder what RCA stands for?"

Back in a bedroom in Manchester with my new secondhand record player. The best place in the world. Never mind Cornwall, it was crap. I bought "John" with my pocket-money and I danced with him, and played it and played it again and (again). I got hold of a ticket for the Hard Rock. I've still got it. My mother wouldn't let me go. I absolutely hated her. She didn't realize, she didn't understand, so the lady bought me some "stardust" and then she did. I absolutely loved her.

The album cover said "to be played at maximum volume"…it was! One thing I remember that totally confused me for a while was why would someone "make love to his eagle?" Well anyway we had a budgie…and I loved that.

"Ziggy this, Ziggy that, Zig Zag Ziggy."

"Why don't you go out and play football?"

"I can't – I've swapped it"…The Boy Who Sold the Ball.

On my birthday in October we went to visit my Nan. I couldn't believe what she got me, she knew I was a fan. It was a "ticker ticker" Timex with a red Bowie strap, a matching Bowie comb case and the first ever picture postcard of "Dave Bowie"…. and I've still got them!

1973

Number 1524, that's what I am, now I'm an official "Dave Bowie" fan. It was football, painting, bird's eggs and Ziggy. And not in that order. I wonder what happened to the Free Trade Hall Gig? I must've been playing out.

Running down the wing with a hedgehog on my head, when I get a bit older I'm gonna dye it red. Off came the eyebrows, on went the glitter, didn't get many jobs as a babysitter.

My schooldays were insane…

"He's a puff that Bowie is, he's a puff."

"So…so f***ing what."

They didn't realize you get more girls that way. Wankers.

I did a morning paper round. Every week I sat down in the entry reading Popswop, Mirabelle and Jackie. I used to rip the Bowie bits out. I got the sack after three weeks.

Summer holiday…

Running round Blackpool Fun Fair I spot two Ziggy posters.

"Oi Mister. What do I 'ave to do?"

"Score under twenty-one with three darts."

"Ok."

First throw…'four', second throw…'eleven', third throw…'two'

"Sixteen! I'll have that Ziggy poster please."

"No it's seventeen."

"F★★★ off. It's under twenty-one, isn't it?"

So I try for the second poster. Could I get under twenty-one again? Could I, bollocks. Seven goes I had, spent all my money…. still only got one poster. The bloke just shrugged his shoulders. I walked off devastated. I went to meet my mum in the ice cream café, she was smiling and waving…she always looked fine.

"What have you won?"

"A Ziggy poster."

"So why are you looking fed up? It's a lovely picture."

"I've spent all my spends and I only won one, there was two of them."

"You spent ALL of your money trying to get the other poster? Right….wait here with your brother."

She came back two minutes later with the other Ziggy poster.

"Thanks Mum, you're great! You got under twenty-one then?"

"No, the man gave it to me."

I don't know how my Mum did things, but she ALWAYS seemed to sort everything out. I found out years later that she threatened to punch the fella because he'd taken all my money. "Wham Bam Thank You Ma'am!"

In with a bullet strikes a red and blue lightning flash…"Aladdin Sane." Or so the story goes it should have been "Love A Lad in Vein." I like to think it's an anagram of "Dad's an Alien."

Bowie Quits reads the headline. I was mortified. My mum said it was all planned out: "He's more like an actor. He's just going to change into another role, you'll see." I didn't believe her.

"Who's that on the cover with Bowie?" asked my mum.

"Twiggy?...Isn't she thin?"

"No wonder she's got a boyfriend called Justin!"

The last track got me worried again... "Where Have All The Good Times Gone"...well, they were just around the corner.

THE MAN WHO THRILLED THE WORLD

Sheva Golkow, USA

$\mathcal{I}$T WAS EARLY 1972, I think. My girlfriend and I were downtown on a Saturday, hanging out where most kids in Philly could be found on the weekend — at Sam Goody's on Chestnut Street — not buying anything, just looking. We noticed a guy near us, older. Probably 17 or 18 to our young 14 years of age. He came over and started talking about music; what we liked, what he liked. We weren't sure why he was talking to us but we were too shy to tell him to go away, or to walk away ourselves.

After a few minutes of general music talk he started babbling about this new musician from England, David Bowie. "This Bowie is unbelievably amazing," the guy told us, "and he's going to be huge. Big as the Beatles — if not bigger." My friend and I looked at each other. Bigger than the Beatles? We were skeptical, but intrigued. At this point he told us we had to hear this Bowie, we had to *see* him.

The guy insisted we accompany him to Jerry's Records a block away. (Do you remember when there were several records stores within blocks of each other? Do you remember record stores?) Please, he said. So we followed him to Jerry's — a store that would soon become one of my favorites and a required stop during every visit downtown.

The guy grabbed two albums from the racks: the UK version of *The Man Who Sold the World* and *Hunky Dory*. "Here he is, here he is!" The guy was practically jumping up and down he was so excited. "Look at him on the cover — he's wearing a dress, isn't that fantastic? He's beautiful, he's beyond male or female, gay or straight — he just *is*; he's the future!" And on and on he went, talking about this incredible singer and his wonderful songs and his amazing presence. I don't remember how the conversation ended; we might have drifted away, or perhaps he just got lost in his reverie and forgot we were there. He never told us his name, and I never saw him again.

I remember looking once more at the albums he'd shown us and wishing I could buy them just to see what it was that had so entranced this guy. But I never had any money in those days. I didn't know that in within a few months' time I'd own *Hunky Dory* as well as *The Rise and Fall of Ziggy Stardust and the Spiders from Mars* and that they'd take up permanent residence on my little plastic record player. I didn't know there would be a whole bunk of girls at camp that summer who swore complete devotion to this magical man. I didn't know that my guitar-playing brother would, for a short time, own a lovely white Fender bass, and that I'd figure out the bass from "Suffragette City" and play it over and over. I didn't know my entire city was going to fall in love with Bowie, that our love would be returned and that the love affair would burn for years — forever.

Thanks mystery guy. And thank you David.

THE GIG THAT CHANGED MY LIFE

Chatham Central Hall —
12 June 1973 — 6:30 pm performance
on the Aladdin Sane Tour
Stuart Dalzell, UK

The Build Up

1973 WAS A DEPRESSING year. At school the pressure was on to get those all-important "O" levels. More than forty years on, the year is still remembered for power cuts, the three-day working week, the oil crisis, and a miners' strike. But for me, it will always stand out as the year I went to my first ever gig — and it was David Bowie!

As a shy, introverted 14 year old my interest in rock 'n' roll had been kindled the previous year with brief flirtations with the scary Alice Cooper and the wonderful T. Rex. However, it was *that* infamous performance of "Starman" on *Top of The Pops* in 1972 which changed everything for me. It's difficult to comprehend the impact and significance that moment in rock history had at the time, especially now as we live in what seems to be more enlightened times. But this was the first time Bowie was able to unleash the androgynous Ziggy Stardust into the unsuspecting living rooms of suburbia —the glam rock bomb had detonated and nothing would be the same again!

The next day at school *everyone* was talking about it...Ziggy had definitely landed!

I bought the *Rise and Fall of Ziggy Stardust* as soon as it was released and loved it, although there was always a part of me who wanted a "rockier" feel. Then "Jean Genie" was released and I thought I'd died and gone to heaven. Mick Rock's promo film with Ziggy, now cast as an "LA Street Urchin," is undoubtedly for me one of Bowie's finest moments and also perfectly showcases the brilliant guitar work of Mick Ronson. It was a classic. I still love it now.

School work could wait – I was hooked!

Aladdin Sane Tour Announcement

In the 1970s the only way to find out about anything was to buy the music papers. I'd eagerly rush to the local news agents every Wednesday morning to snap up *New Musical Express*, *Melody Maker* and *Sounds* and pick through each page, hoping to find any snippet of news about Bowie.

It wasn't long before my efforts were rewarded. Bowie would embark on a huge UK tour in May and June to promote a new album *Aladdin Sane*, and to my amazement, he was coming to Chatham — just down the road!!!

Happy Days. The next hurdle was to secure tickets.

There were no internet bookings, phone apps, call centers, etc – this was 1973 after all. You just had to go to the venue and pay, cheque or cash. We'd already run the box office and been told that tickets were going on sale at 10 am the following Saturday. There were rumours that the Coop Travel Agent in Gravesend would also have an allocation, but this mission was far too critical to leave anything to chance. We had already been thrown into a state of panic as the abrupt lady on the end of the phone had suggested we get to the box office early as there might be a big queue! We needed to plan our ticket strategy with military precision. Failing was not an option!

Getting Tickets

I had recruited my best mate, Chris, to come along with me to get tickets. We left on the 8:30 am train from Gravesend to Chatham. We arrived to a damp Chatham High Street at around 9 am where we were greeted by a meandering queue of about 100 other space oddities. But all was good. The panic eased as we realized the venue held over 1200. As we approached the two small windows of the box office, I retrieved my £2.20 — "two tickets in the balcony please"— I was elated to see we were handed row A.

We'd opted for the special matinee show at 6:30 pm as we didn't want to be roaming the streets of Chatham late on a Tuesday evening dressed in our best space invader outfits. We had specifically chosen the balcony as we were unsure how "rowdy" the front stalls might become. New to all this as such, this rock 'n' roll virgin felt much happier elevated above the mayhem of the stalls, especially as my mate was barely 4 foot 11 inches! We'd done it! We had our tickets and we were going to see Bowie live! I was so thrilled I kept my ticket obsessively flat under plastic in an old photo album. I had to keep it in pristine condition.

In the run up to the gig there had been some bad reviews of the opening night at Earl's Court. Bowie was the first artist to play this huge concrete box of a venue and had underestimated the problems with the sound. A second gig on 30th May at the same venue was subsequently cancelled. It was an embarrassing disaster.

"A Lad in Distress" the headline of *Melody Maker* proclaimed. Oh dear.

Then, only a few weeks later we were treated to a hilarious BBC Nationwide news item on early evening TV. Bernard Falk, I believe, was the "outraged" reporter.

The BBC had sent a crew to film the show and fans in Bournemouth. In a shocking revelation, we were informed that Bowie used makeup on stage and would undoubtedly corrupt the youth of Britain with his bizarre stage antics — a sort of a "lock up your daughters (and your sons)" hysteria.

All this frenzied reporting just made us more excited — roll on June 12th!

The Concert

Getting to the venue was again planned with military precision. The "dads" had been recruited with strict instructions concerning drop off and pick up times. There would be no public transport tonight, especially with those platform shoes! We arrived at the venue where several hundred fellow fans were already waiting for the doors to open. Various unsavoury characters paraded up and down with arms full of unofficial posters and other cheap merchandise. Once inside I bought everything: badges, programs and even a dayglow scarf!

We found our seats and settled in ready for the show. The venue smelt of tobacco and stale beer, and the seats were the spring loaded cinema type, covered in stained and faded red velvet. We were happy — row A meant a clear unrestricted view of the stage and also all the colorful fans in the front stalls! We could clearly see the drum kit with "The Spiders" spelt out in large adhesive letters and a giant "Aladdin Sane" lightning flash hung as a backdrop.

We were ready.

The famous Clockwork Orange march started booming

through the speaker stack. You could feel the excitement. Two girls in the front stalls started screaming, and then suddenly, centre stage was Bowie with arms outstretched. The spotlight hit him as Ronson and the Spiders hammered into the opening chords of "Hang Onto Yourself." I had never heard anything as loud! It was sensory overload, the stunning visuals and the volume so huge my seat was shaking. *Wow*! I loved it!

Bowie ran through a great selection of old and new tracks, many from *Aladdin Sane*. The costume changes kept coming, with stage hands all in black suddenly running on stage and simply pulling one costume off to reveal an even more exotic Japanese creation underneath.

Rock 'n' Roll had never seen anything like this and neither had Chatham. The treats kept coming – one of the highlights being an extended version of "Width of a Circle" with Bowie experimenting with mime. You could feel that imaginary wall Bowie had suddenly created in the middle of the stage. Amazing.

The show was truly mind blowing. The only slight disappointment was that "Cracked Actor" had been cut from the set list, presumably because of the deadline for the 8:30 pm show. It seems unbelievable now that Bowie was playing two shows a night at some venues.

The show finished and we left shell shocked. The crowd for the later show was gathered in the street, more hard core than the previous. The heels were higher and the hair dye brighter! I wrapped my dayglow scarf around my neck and headed home with great memories and ringing ears.

The Aftermath

Nothing would ever be the same after that gig. I so wanted to see the show again and had read that final dates at the Hammersmith Odeon had been added to the schedule. All I had to do was convince a fellow school mate to come along to the show on Tuesday 3rd July, however that proved impossible as it was a math homework night. I gave up and resigned myself I'd have to wait until Ziggy toured again.

Nobody realized how important the Hammersmith show would become in the history of rock 'n' roll. Bowie killed off Ziggy but I had at least been privileged to see him just that once.

I wanted to recreate the excitement of that Bowie gig, so I religiously scoured the music press to see who was touring, and much to my delight it wasn't long before another of Bowie's protégés, Mott the Hoople, were coming to Chatham supported by an up and coming rock band called "Queen" — this would be my second gig! In hindsight, my gig CV now looks very impressive. The show was fantastic, but it wasn't Bowie.

My craving for more live Bowie led me to hunt out the elusive bootlegs. "Bowie Joins the Bootleg Brigade" announced an intriguing headline in *NME*. It was a detailed review of the now legendary *Santa Monica* double bootleg LP on the Trade Mark of Quality label. I had to get this! I'd seen an ad in the classified of *Melody Maker* — World Records: Rare and Live Recordings. They were based in San Francisco so I sent off an international reply coupon (you had to buy from a post office) to a mysterious box office number and soon received a catalogue.

I could barely contain my excitement as I read the Bowie listings — *In Person In America* (aka *Santa Monica 72*) double album, *All American Bowie* (Long Beach Arena), *His Master's Voice* (final Hammersmith gig). I bought them all and played them to death! I thought that listening to them would surely be the only way I'd be able to relive the experience of Bowie in concert. Bowie had retired, so that meant no more gigs???

After three long years, Bowie finally announced a week residency in May 1976 at the Empire Pool Wembley (now renamed Wembley Arena). The drought was over — I went every night. But that's a story for another time.

THE GLITTER YEARS

Jackie Miles, UK

"WHY HAVE YOU COME to school looking like this?" demanded the Head Mistress.

"It was Ziggy Stardust Miss." I went on to explain, "I was paying homage to Ziggy Stardust — he's an alien rock star."

I had shaved off my eyebrows and painted a gold circle on my forehead, which had resulted in lunchtime detention for a whole week and earned me the label "Bowie freak." These days I'm sure I would have been called a "free-thinking individual," but it was the early 1970s and I was in a very strict all-girls school where it was considered radical if you rolled up your school skirt above the knee.

My earliest recollection of David Bowie was when my older sister brought home the original acoustic single of "Space Oddity." Whilst listening to this on our portable record player and in the total darkness of our bedroom, we did a "Lost in Space" dance routine which involved standing on our beds, arms outstretched swaying wildly to convey hopelessness.

In 1972 when the Ziggy Stardust album was released, it was like a revelation to me; as if this alien being had suddenly landed in our midst and was beckoning us to join him. On the record itself was a warning to our parents: "TO BE PLAYED AT MAXIMUM VOLUME"

The posters of Ziggy in his knitted one-piece that appeared in my *Jackie* magazines caused much consternation among my friends who were into David Cassidy and Donny Osmond and they desperately tried to dissuade me from being a Bowie fan. By then it was too late, as I was well and truly hooked. I hated those clean living American pop stars — Bowie was different and shocking, which to me as a rebellious teenager was very appealing.

I had the coolest haircut in the school which I styled myself using my Dad's best Gillette razor. I found this to be the ideal implement for recreating the Ziggy "feather cut" as it was known then. Other kids at school would regularly call at my house for me to give them the Ziggy make over and I often wonder how on earth my Dad managed to get a good shave in those days as his razor must have been permanently blunt.

My biggest regret to this day is not having seen David Bowie as Ziggy. Living in darkest Suffolk at the time, where a notice was pinned on a tree if a disco was to take place at the weekend, there was no way he was ever going to play here. However, my chance came in 1976 when the Station to Station tour was announced. In those days there was no internet so it was a case of completing a coupon from the *Melody Maker*, sending it off with a postal order and then waiting (and hoping) for about six weeks for the tickets to arrive.

I can still remember the day very clearly. It was just as exciting hanging around outside Wembley Arena watching the Bowie clones parading in all their finery as it was to be my first Bowie gig.

A photographer approached my cousin and I and asked us to pose for some photographs for a fashion magazine, which we did quite willingly. After pouting at the camera for several minutes, we found that he was taking pictures of our silver shoes.

Inside the arena Beethoven's Ninth was playing as we made

our way to our seats and an old black and white film called
Un Chien Andalou by Salvador Dali was projected on a silver
screen. Our allocated seats were way back from the stage.
Unfortunately, sitting directly in front of me, was Jordan the
punk who was causing quite a stir in her black rubber cat
suit. She had styled her hair into an enormous beehive which
obscured much of my view throughout most of the performance!
The atmosphere was electric with anticipation when the impossibly
long intro to "Station to Station" started and then after what
seemed like forever, from a dark corner of the stage, I heard a
familiar voice sing "the return of the thin white duke" and there
he was: a tiny speck on the stage in an entirely black and white
stark set, save for his flame coloured hair. It was a truly memorable
moment and one I shall treasure always.

Over all too soon, we joined the throngs of Bowie fans on the
tube making our way home in quiet reflection and studying our
copies of the Isolar tour programme — all wondering what Kirlian
photography was but not daring to ask. We had seen Bowie and
life was never going to be boring again.

THE STORY OF SIGMA SOUND & THE SIGMA KIDS

Patti Brett, USA

$\mathcal{O}$N AUGUST 1974, OVER the course of two weeks, David Bowie recorded *Young Americans* at Sigma Sound Studios in Philadelphia. The story of Bowie inviting ten lucky fans into the studio has become somewhat legendary in the Bowie world. This is the story of how I became one of the "Sigma Kids."

In July 1974, David Bowie played six shows at the Tower Theater, in Upper Darby, Pennsylvania, to promote his *Diamond Dogs* album. We camped out for the concert tickets in May and were rewarded with mostly front row pit tickets for the shows. As the week became reality, we went to the shows but would leave as soon as the shows were over and head off to David's hotel, The Bellevue Stratford on Broad Street. One of the nights, David sat out on the front steps of the hotel and chatted with about ten or so of us. He told us he would be recording a new album in August at Sigma Sound Studios and that we should look for him.

A few short weeks later, not knowing exactly when he was to arrive at the studio, we started to drive by to see if we saw any activity. Finally, a friend drove by and saw his car outside (a blue Cadillac limo with New York plates). We immediately started hanging out at the studio to catch a glimpse of our idol! Now remember, these are the pre-cell phone and pre-internet days, but word spread like wildfire; there were often a couple of dozen kids making 12th Street their temporary residence — in the middle of Skid Row.

We got to see David come out of the studio and we followed him back to his hotel. This time he was staying at the Barclay Hotel, on posh Rittenhouse Square where our vigil/routine would begin each day at around 4 or 5 pm. David would come out of the hotel and chat with everyone waiting for him. Photos were taken, autographs signed and he would get into his limo and be off to the studio for the night. We would jump in our cars as soon as he headed to his and run every red light on the way, so we could be waiting at the studio as he arrived. There would often be different people at the hotel that didn't go to the studio and vice versa. A small group of us always did both. The same scenario ensued at the end of each studio session.

Since we were always around as the band members were headed out and in, we became friendly with most of them. We would drive the band to places all over town; tell them where to go to find things, where to grab a quick bite to eat and more. One day, we even got to take Stuey, David's bodyguard, record shopping! We became fast friends with the affable Carlos Alomar, his lovely wife Robin Clark and their dear friend Luther Vandross. They were just a few years older than most of us, but they took us under their wing, like Mom and Dad would. Some nights, after the recording sessions, Carlos and Robin would invite us to their hotel room and play cassettes of what they had recorded that evening. We also convinced the guys that worked at the studio to open a window that was behind the glass, next to the sound board, so we could hear what was going on upstairs in Studio A.

Often, while waiting outside the studio, we would convince David's driver, Jimmy James, to let us into the limo, where we would steal cigarette butts (always *Gitanes*) and red David hairs off the back seat of the car. We also got to be acquainted with Angie, David's wife, and little Zowie, their son. We cultivated a friendly relationship with both Tony Visconti, David's producer and Coco Schwab, David's personal assistant. Things were going quite well and everyone was having a great time!

One night, as David went into the studio, he said, "If you are still out here when I come out, I have a surprise for you." I knew I wasn't going anywhere! When David left the studio that night, there were just a handful of us outside. He said, "You've all been so wonderful and supportive to us while we've been here. We should be finishing laying down the tracks in the next couple of days. I want to invite you to come up into the studio when we finish and listen to what we've done. Don't tell anyone, just you that are here now. Keep it under your hat," at which point he lifted his fedora and put it back down.

Coco let us know the day before the auspicious event was to take place and reminded us not to mention it to anyone else or it wasn't going to happen. It was a Thursday night, into Friday, and there were loads of people waiting to catch sight of David going into the studio. David had arranged for a photographer to document the event and those of us that were to be taken upstairs were all dressed up. People that were just hanging around wondered why we were so dressed up, but we kept our promise. We weren't telling anyone what was about to happen, but we had to get rid of them before this could take place. The photographer, Dagmar, was shooting us doing a variety of things: running down the street, spelling out the word Bowie with our bodies, and listening at the above mentioned window.

Eventually, we convinced the hangers-on that they didn't really need to stay and that David wouldn't be out for hours upon hours and they should just go home, as we were planning to do. One by one, they all left until it was just us. Sometime around midnight, a light rain started to fall. Somehow word got to David who asked that we be let into the first floor lobby while we waited.

Finally! Coco came down and escorted us upstairs to the interior of Studio A. David was behind the glass at the soundboard. We sat down and David said over the microphone, "So what you are going to listen to is what we've been working on the last two weeks. It's very rough, we just finished laying down the tracks and there is quite a bit of work to still be done, but you will get the idea. It's so very different than anything I've ever done and I hope you like it." He then came out into the studio with us and the band and took a seat in the back. David rocked back and forth, chewing on his fingernails, anxiously awaiting our response. We were all so in awe of what was taking place, none of us were able to move, let alone speak!

At the end of the playback, one of the kids yelled out, "Play it again!" David got a huge grin on his face and said, "Really"? We all screamed "YES!" At this point, the tension broke and David got up and danced, chatted and became more at home with us being there. We had such a good time with him, it was almost as if we were part of his band or at least his peers and not just fans.

Unfortunately, the time came for us to leave. We said our goodbyes (they were leaving town the next day), everyone hugged and got kisses. Coco took down all our names and addresses and David promised us tickets to the show coming up in November (which he did get for us). Somewhere along the line, a writer for one of the local newspapers must have been around because they printed the story of our good fortune in the Sunday paper.

When the shows in November came along, we were all in the front, basking in our new found closeness to our idol who had become our friend. He looked down at us dozens of times during the show, beaming at us. At some point after that tour, he began to search for us at shows, asking where his "Sigma Kids" were. He always found us and we always remembered, for a few short hours, we were as close to our hero and idol as if we were part of the family. *Sigma Kids.* Forever.

AND MY LIFE
WAS CHANGED

A RAINY AFTERNOON
IN PHILADELPHIA
Mark W. Falzini, USA

I'M A RELATIVELY NEW-COMER to the world of David Bowie fandom. I became a fan on September 6, 1996. That was the day I went with a friend to see my first Bowie concert. She had been a life-long fan and I could never quite understand why someone her age was willing to travel to God-knows-where and stand in line for God-knows-how-long to listen to this person sing. So when she invited me to tag along to a concert, I thought it would be a good chance to conduct an anthropological/sociological study. She said that, if I liked it, she would take me to a concert in New York City a week or so later. Convinced I wouldn't like the concert, she arranged for my sister to go to the New York show instead.

We arrived in Philadelphia at the Electric Factory in the afternoon and stood outside in a light rain. When we got inside, lo and behold, no seats. I was not happy — I wanted to sit down! Oh well. So I start to look around at the crowd that was smooshed in the smallish room. I was shocked at both the number of people and the span of ages — young kids to "old people," senior citizens even! Just what was going on?

My back was aching.

Finally, Bowie came out on stage. The crowd erupted. Then it happened. He started to sing. I could not believe what I was hearing. I swear it was on the first note out of his mouth that I became a "die-hard fan."

My sister never got to go to the New York concert. I attended fourteen more (including his 50th birthday concert at Madison Square Garden) before he stopped touring in 2004.

Like everyone else, I'm very grateful to Bowie for his catalog of incredible music. But for me it was more than the music. It was...is...the people. It was through Bowie, his concerts and fan websites, that I've met some of my closest friends around the world. The Earthling Tour in 1997 was one of the most exciting times in my life. The months leading up to the tour involved scores of his fans gathering on the *Teenage Wildlife* fan page chat room. We all discussed where we were going to be seeing him and as the concerts happened, we raced home to post the set lists. We made arrangements to "meet up" with our on-line friends at the shows. Somehow, I was able to convince my parents to allow a fellow fan from Sweden to come and stay with us so he could attend the shows here on the east coast with me. We would wait in line for hours and hours before the show. Sometimes I think waiting in line was more fun that the concert! We all "knew" each other from the chatroom so it became a huge tailgate party of sorts. I ended up seeing Bowie five times in a two week period during that tour, traveling to Philadelphia, Washington DC and New York City.

Since then I've been fortunate to attend several more concerts and to travel abroad to finally meet in person many of my on-line "Bowie friends." I've been to see them several times and some have been here to visit me. Interestingly, we rarely discussed Bowie when we got together, instead focusing on each other and our lives (but with Bowie playing in the background!). I'm happy to say that they have become and remain some of my closest and most important friends. We became more than just "Bowie friends"; we've become *real* friends, sharing in each other's "real life" joys and sorrows.

I learned of David Bowie's death at 5:00 in the morning when I woke up as my cell phone exploded with texts, emails and Facebook messages from my friends around the world. "Bowie friends" and others — wanting to make sure I knew the news. While I am mourning the loss of this incredible musician, I'm also smiling as I think of all the experiences and friends he has made possible for me. It's amazing the impact a musician has had on the past twenty years of my life.

And it all started with a concert on a rainy afternoon in Philadelphia.

BOWIE DROPPED INTO MY LIFE

Barbara Streun, Germany

$\mathcal{O}$WISH I HAD SOME story to tell — some funny event or Bowie related adventure. Of course there are some funny stories about our trips to Bowie shows all over Europe, but they would only be about his travelling fans. I had always hoped to meet him one day. Maybe pretending not to recognize him or act like a fan. But just to have the opportunity to talk — human being to human being. That never happened. Nevertheless, Bowie and I — there indeed is a kind of story. It's about how Bowie became my secret companion and dropped into my life when I most needed him.

I always knew there was someone called "David Bowie" and I liked some of his music. Until I was in my twenties, I bought most of his records and added them to my collection. I liked him, but was not a "fan." In general, after a childhood of being a Beatles fan, my interest in pop music had declined over the years. Maybe I thought I was too old to be a fan. But sometimes things can change very quickly!

When *Heathen* was released in early 2002, I had a look at the German Bowie website for more information. Yes, let's blame it on the internet! I went there again and again because the Bowie fans I met in that virtual reality were mostly rather interesting people. Bowie played a legendary concert in Cologne in July 2002. I did not even try to get a ticket. At that time I never would have considered travelling to another city for a concert. After that show, I read such a great report on the web that when Bowie announced more shows later that year I bought a ticket for Berlin. Later, I also got a ticket for Munich! How quickly things change.

September 22, 2002 was the day when I saw Bowie live for the first time in my life. When he appeared on stage it totally blew me away! I became a member of *Bowienet* and got to know people from all over the world. I went to see Bowie shows throughout Europe. And I was one of the lucky ones who won a ticket for the "Riverside" concert in September 2003. Life started to be very exciting again and quite different from what I had ever expected!

Being a Bowie fan is much more than just buying and listening to records. Many of the Bowie people are very creative artists. Bowie always was a big inspiration, encouraging us to be creative ourselves. I never heard of a Bowie fan being sued for copyright issues or forced to close their website, and my *"Bowiefun"* website was always allowed to stay. But most important is the music. Sometimes you need time, even years, to understand certain songs. And then they just touch your heart and soul — as if sharing frequencies as they resonate within. Most Bowie fans share this sense. Even more, Bowie's bright mind, sense of humor, knowledge and wisdom helped me take an interest in things besides music. It was a time when I was bored and pretty fed up with university, jobs and most of the role models I had grown up with. I had lost my curiosity over the years and Bowie helped me to find it again.

I was in the audience in Prague when Bowie cut short a show in 2004, and then stopped the tour a few days later. All was very quiet the following years. But it was enough to know he was on the planet and hopefully enjoying his reclusive life.

In 2007, I went to the "High Line Festival" in New York City.

Finally, my Bowie devotion made me go to New York City — a place I had always wanted to visit. It was fun. Bowie was sitting in the cinema just two rows behind us watching the movie *El Automovil Gris*. Of course, our attention for the movie was a bit spoiled.

In 2013, the release of "Where Are We Now" was such a surprise and had such special meaning for me. My mother died in April 2014 from cancer after being ill for nearly two years. During her last weeks as I took care of her and felt overwhelmed, I listed to "Where Are We Now" in an endless loop at night with my headphones. It felt like Bowie had written this just for me — our whole world is changing when someone we love is passing away. We wake up and wonder where we are now. *"The stars look very different today..."*

I will always be grateful to Mr. Bowie for his last gift to the world that is *Blackstar*. It is so much more than just another "record." Full of despair and fear but also solace, gratitude and showing us a way to deal with the inevitable that we all must face.

I will never forget that Bowie smile just four weeks before his passing. I was among the few fans in New York City, waiting in front of the theater at the premiere of *Lazarus*. As we now know, he was terminally ill — and yet, that beaming Bowie smile.

I hope that Bowie found what he was hoping for in eternity.

HOW DAVID BOWIE TAUGHT US TO WELCOME OUR NEXT DAYS

Daniel F. Le Ray, USA

$\mathscr{B}$OWIE HELPED ME — helped us all — *become*. Creating is always becoming. You could reinvent yourself and become someone new; you could wear a skin-tight leotard or a shirt and waistcoat; you could be gay, queer, straight, it didn't matter; you could be glam, soul, ambient, pop, or industrial and you were always becoming you.

There are some things that I know for certain. If I hadn't become a Bowie fan:

1. I would probably not have learned to play the guitar as quickly as I did;
2. I would probably not have suggested that we name a dog "Ziggy;"
3. I would probably have come much later if at all to: Christopher Isherwood, Orwell, the Velvet Underground, Warhol, Pixies, my passing but ever-present interests in style, design and clothes, Aleister Crowley, Jean Genet, *A Clockwork Orange*, Anthony Newley, T. Rex or Scott

Walker, Iggy and the Stooges, Ryuichi Sakamoto, *Baal* and *The Threepenny Opera*, "Alabama Song," Hanif Kureishi, the Übermensch, *Stranger in a Strange Land* or William S. Burroughs;

4. I would probably not have such a love of the "meta" and self-referentiality in literature, art, movies, and music;

5. I would certainly not have used a Bowie reference as my first ever email password;

6. I would certainly not have written a song in response to "Changes" called "Everything Stays the Same" or a short story called "Standing By The Wall;"

7. I would absolutely, certainly, not have created Warhol-style screen prints featuring repeated images of Bowie in secondary school art class;

8. I would absolutely, certainly, definitely not have reconnected with a school friend after university, formed a short-lived David Bowie tribute band named Hot Tramp, then performed only Bowie songs at several open mic nights using guitars, harmonicas, and a children's glockenspiel; and

I know I wouldn't be quite the same person I am now — intellectually or creatively.

Excerpt from the original article which appeared in *The Huffington Post*, 2016.

BOWIE AND I

Julie Stoller, USA

I'M GLAD I KEPT my old scrapbooks. Because every time I want to remember, I can just drag them out and dust them off, and then it all feels current again.

For a true epiphany to occur, there is usually an auspicious joining of circumstance, time and place. My Bowie awakening occurred when I returned home to Connecticut after a three-year misguided adventure in Florida that was accompanied by an endless soundtrack of tired, bland Southern rock. I was burnt out and at a spiritual dead end. My salvation came in the form of a young Bowie fan at a technical school we were both attending, and he introduced me (or rather *reintroduced* me) to the music and artistic vision of David Bowie. It was a complete departure from where I had just been. I was entranced.

This was in 1982, just before *Let's Dance*. I was obviously very late to the game, but I wasted no time and immersed myself completely.

My first Bowie concerts were his two shows in Hartford, Connecticut during the 1983 Serious Moonlight Tour. While *Let's Dance* wasn't a favorite, that happened to be my timing. For the first show, my young guide and I dressed as our favorite Bowie characters. He was the aloof Thin White Duke, while I was a

cross between the misunderstood space alien and a white-faced
mute mime. That says it all, really. I graduated, he dropped out
and disappeared from my life, but my newfound Bowie fandom
took off into the stratosphere. As I tend to do with my Scorpio
nature, I became obsessed.

As my devotion grew, I gravitated toward the *Low/Heroes/
Lodger* trilogy — especially *Low*. There was something about
that sense of isolation, the constant searching and yearning, the
endless endeavors and failings, not feeling quite right in one's own
skin — that I instantly identified with. I've always felt like I was
outside of the mainstream, and Bowie bestowed his blessing on all
of us who were trying to forge our own way, through uncharted
lands. He was our shining beacon, our knowledgeable guide, our
mystical Sherpa.

Other David Bowie albums that will always be close to my
heart include *Space Oddity (Man of Words, Man of Music), The
Man Who Sold The World* and *Hunky Dory*, plus the very early
song, "Conversation Piece." *TMWSTW,* with its unsettling music
and lyrics that spoke of mental illness, deeply resonated with
me. "Width of a Circle" was a song I understood on a visceral
level, having lived with bipolar disorder in my family. I later
learned that the album was inspired by Bowie's half-brother Terry,
who suffered from schizophrenia. The cheery/wistful songs on
Space Oddity and *Hunky Dory* overflowed with equal amounts of
vulnerability and youthful optimism — something I also identified
with. "Conversation Piece" put into sharp focus the idea of being
alone and alienated in a crowded world. It was all a revelation.
Here was a kindred spirit.

In a continuous wave of serendipity, I began meeting fellow
fans, collectors, minor legends and all sorts of fascinating characters.
In was a Felliniesque odyssey. Just before Bowie's Glass Spider
album and tour, I started a newsletter with longtime Bowie fan
Rose Winters, who collaborated with the legendary fan David

Jeffrey Fletcher on *David Robert Jones Bowie: the discography of a generalist, 1962-1979*. Our humble photocopied newsletter was called *Bowie Bits*, which then morphed into the formally printed (and ridiculously pricey) *Sound & Vision*. For about 5 years, we served up news, rumors, reviews, personal fan stories, a few interviews with Bowie celebrities like Mick Rock and Rykodisc's Jeff Rougvie and a collector's trading post. Ah, those quaint pre-blog days!

And then there were the concerts — oh god, the concerts! From arenas in the Northeastern US in 1983 to massive festival crowds in 1987, mostly outdoors, in Holland, Belgium, Germany, Italy, England, Sweden, Austria, France and Spain. I attended exciting exclusive press conferences on both sides of the pond, a scrappy Tin Machine show at a dodgy club called The World on New York's Lower East Side and another intimate gathering on their next tour at the tiny Toad's Place in New Haven. There was an improbable "Sound & Vision Fan Convention" in Los Angeles, loosely based around a Tin Machine live taping at LAX for an *In Concert* TV broadcast. It was a whirlwind of nutty adventures with friends in a kaleidoscope of cities, while I was corresponding and trading with fans all over the world. The memories (and half dozen scrapbooks) are just as much of the interesting people I met as they are of the man's music, all part of the same glorious experience.

I dropped out of the Bowie fandom to focus on other things and pulled away from a few albums that didn't speak to me as much, but came back for Earthling and pretty much stayed, though appreciating the music in a quieter, more personal way. *The Next Day* and *Blackstar* were revelations, as compelling and life-altering for me as *Low* was back when I first heard it. It has often been said that Bowie, throughout his career, has been holding up a mirror to our civilization. I think he has also been shining a strong light into the future, daring us to follow it.

In addition to exploring Bowie's oeuvre, his considerable influence in my life continues to make itself felt in subtle ways, such as a recent decision to ditch the computer work I hated and focus on writing again. It's about not being afraid to go down a less traveled road, even in the face of uncertainty. This requires a celebration of one's own strangeness and a full embrace of who you were meant to be — in addition to valuing this uniqueness in others. With that as a signpost, I continue an undeterred, never-ending inquiry.

Thank you, David. You've left us one hell of a legacy.

A REALITY TOUR
Kathryn Kopple, USA

"*Y*OUR FATHER HAS DIED" has to be one of the worst wake-up calls. Mine came around midnight. A woman's voice — calm and apologetic — preamble: "*Is this Kathryn? We have you down as your father's emergency contact? Kathryn, I am sorry to have to tell you this….*"

Seven weeks after receiving this news, I flew from Philadelphia to Los Angeles to see Bowie play at the Wiltern LG Theater. It was a flight from *lie down and never get up again* grief to "Oh! You Pretty Things." Or at least I was hoping Bowie would play "Oh! You Pretty Things." It's one of my all-time favorites. It's also the kind of song that gets fans thinking. They describe the song as apocalyptic, pulp science fiction, gothic, youthfully rebellious. From the sound of it, fans don't think of "Oh! You Pretty Things" as a happy song. They pay it due respect but it is almost universally acknowledged as pretty much full of doom and gloom. And so was I. The death of my father confused and terrified me. Many days, in a state of excruciating anxiety, I was certain I, too, was dying.

And then, a few weeks after the saddest call of my life, I received another call. It was a close friend of mine, Frank. We had met years ago, and he had since moved to Hollywood. We still stayed in touch, talking on the phone most days. On that particular day, he called to tell me Bowie was coming. "*Where?*"

Philadelphia, I hoped. But no, he was playing in California. I remember thinking I couldn't go — kids, husband, time, money. Frank said that I had to go. Frank knew how much Bowie meant to me. He loved Bowie too. Seeing Bowie together, especially at a great venue like the Wiltern, would be beyond wonderful. I asked Frank to give me the dates. *"Next week,"* he said. Actually, it was less than a week.

Without Bowie, the chances were slim that Frank and I would have become friends. I met Frank when he was working at a video store (remember those?) and I was a suburban housewife expecting her first child. Six months into my pregnancy, in my usual sleep-deprived, pre-partum haze, I stopped by the store. Going in, I could hear Bowie's voice. I looked around. On one of the monitors, there he was: David Bowie, in all his greatness and beauty. From the time I saw him perform on *The Midnight Special* as Ziggy Stardust right up to the moment I walked into the video store, Bowie always knocked me out. I revered him. As for Frank, he was behind the counter singing along. I told him it was nice to meet another person who liked Bowie. He responded, *"Oh My God!"* Just like that, we became Bowie friends.

The thing about Bowie friends is they never let you down. Or at least Frank never let me down. He kept me in the Bowie loop, always looking out for album releases, tours, news. He became my connection to Bowie — channeling Bowie for me at a time when raising my kids pretty much subsumed me. When my father died, my youngest was only a year old. He was named Alexander, after my father. I told Frank I couldn't leave Alex. Frank told me to get David (my husband) to take care of the kids. Loaded down with depression and responsibilities, my mantra was *I can't, I can't, I can't.* For every *I can't,* Frank talked me through, making me understand that there would be no regrets. I was going to see Bowie.

To this day, I swear Bowie, by his sheer presence, lifted me from the from the grimy catacombs where I grappled with my father's death and placed me on a pink cloud. The concert rocked. I doubt there was a person in the house who wasn't bowled over. There were these two women, total strangers, who befriended me when I told them I had flown in from Philadelphia to see Bowie play. Along with Frank they became my concert buddies. When Bowie kicked off the concert with "Rebel, Rebel" they hugged me and we began to dance. We held hands during "Heroes." We couldn't stop cheering when Bowie came back for the encore and played "Ziggy Stardust." During it all, Frank would look over at me, the biggest smile on his face. He had been right. It was a Bowie concert for the ages.

Bowie sang a good number of his best-loved songs that night, but "Oh! you Pretty Things" wasn't part of the set list. I just mention the song, because there is so much about it that reminds me of my father. He was an unusual person — undeniably creative and questioning. He was never resigned to life on earth, not if it meant being shackled to the mundane and dreary reality he saw all around him. Once, I said to him: "Dad, why can't you just be like everyone else? Live an ordinary life?" He smiled — he had such a warm smile — and said: "Nope, I just can't do it." That was my dad, the man who questioned everything. He had landed in the wrong place, century, plane — what have you. And he knew it.

As for Bowie…it was a concert for the ages.

IF I HAD A TIME MACHINE

Alyssa Linn Palmer, Canada

Bowie's death gutted me. A friend had sent me the news via Facebook message, and I opened it that morning with no idea what it would be. The breath left me. I grabbed at the kitchen counter to slow my collapse as my knees weakened. And I sobbed. The world hadn't ended, but the man, the rock star, the actor who meant so much to me was no more.

My first memory of David Bowie was, like so many of my age group (particularly female), that of Jareth the Goblin King, tormenting a youthful Jennifer Connelly. *Labyrinth* is still a favorite film, but for half a dozen years after watching it often, I had yet to realize that its main villain was anything more than an actor. I was twelve or thirteen when that happened, in the early 90s. I devoured biographies, scoured my city library's tape and LP collections…anything I could find. This was pre-internet, of course.

Once the internet arrived, one of the first things I searched for was Bowie, using a text-based browser and coming across a website on Stanford.edu, choosing one picture, a Thin White Duke, to download (which took ages). That site, The David Bowie File, turned into *Teenage Wildlife*. Without the Internet, I wouldn't have found so many other fans and had so many amazing experiences. I would have been stuck in my hometown, wondering where all the other Bowie fans were. But because of the Internet, and *Teenage Wildlife*, and the early *BowieNet*, I know so many others and am still friends with my first Bowie online friends.

In 1995 I bought *1. Outside*, the first Bowie album I'd been able to purchase on release day. Since then, I haven't missed one. Bowie's music has been the soundtrack to my life, taking me through childhood, adolescence, and into my mid-thirties. His interests provoked my own, sending me on tangents and down rabbit holes. I credit him with further expanding my literary knowledge.

And there was nothing like a live Bowie show to get the blood rushing, the adrenaline pumping, the delight taking over my entire being. It wasn't just about the albums or the songs, it was his entire presence. Vancouver on September 6, 1997 was a revelation, the first show of the Earthling tour on its North American leg, and my very first show, age 17. I saw six shows altogether, including two in New York in 2000, one in 2002 in New York again, and two during the Reality tour (in Calgary and Edmonton). If I had a time machine, I'd go back and see many, many more.

As the year rolls on and we come ever closer to what would have been Bowie's 70th birthday, and the one-year marker of his passing, I am grateful and thankful that he did what he did, sharing his creativity and ideas with the world and making such a mark upon my life.

www.alyssalinnpalmer.com.

FROM LABYRINTH
TO LAZARUS

Melanie Krichel, Germany

$\mathscr{T}$HE MOST POWERFUL WORKS of art that enter our lives are those
we have somehow always known. It may be nostalgia at work, or
just the wish to have something in common with a new source
of inspiration; the strongest connection is always the one where
we realize:

"You have been a part of me before."

That was what I thought when Bowie music, inevitably it
seems, came to me shortly after the release of *The Next Day*. In
a way, I was a *Labyrinth* child, from the generation of kids who
grew up dreaming of encounters with Jareth the Goblin King, half
magical creature, half a dancing man with questionable aesthetics.
Even then, I was younger than most *Labyrinth* children, too young
yet to romanticize the fabulous villain from the movie.

However, he stuck with me until about twenty years later,
while purely by chance watching the *Top of The Pops* "Starman"
performance, I realized that he had always been there. As I slowly
familiarized myself with his work, it was incidentally the first time
I was listening to music for music's sake. I had drawn inspiration

for myself and whatever art I was working on, but I had never been as awestruck by music as when I heard "Station to Station."

I had missed the release of *The Next Day* completely, but there was much to discover. Fortunately, I found my way to RaMoana's radio show, and with that to the most inspiring as well as hilarious group of Bowie fans. Three hazy years of interpreting lyrics and listening to an overwhelming amount of live Bowie music passed. Of course, there was always hope that I would be able to see yet another new album release, this time with my own eyes instead of hearing stories of times past.

When *Lazarus* was announced, I was determined to experience it firsthand. I was unspeakably lucky to be welcomed to American by my Bowie mentors, knowing that we were going to be one of the first to hear the newest *Lazarus* songs, performed by the cast. Eventually, I did see the release of *Blackstar* with my own eyes, an experience very different to discovering old music through the cultivated connotations of others. For three blissful days, *Blackstar* felt like something that was made only for me from the breathtaking "Lazarous" to the haunting "go go go go" in "Girl Loves Me." When Monday came, *Blackstar* turned out to be proof of the mastery with which he led his life and his art. I was in awe and in tears, just like those who had grown in his presence and influence for decades.

I am quite sure many *Labyrinth* children feel the same: even though we did not know him for very long, he has reordered time, turned the world upside down and he's done it all for us.

Don't believe for just one second we're forgetting you.

A PLACE IN MY LIFE
Lisa Taylor, UK

$\mathcal{I}$ SNOOZED MY ALARM AROUND 6:50 am. I didn't want to get up.
I eventually woke as my "whatsapp" tone went off on the phone
and this made me realize everyone else was up and about. It was
my friend Morgan. She wrote me a simple message that made me
sick to my stomach. I didn't quite understand or believe it at first.
It read:

Bud I'm so sorry: Bowie RIP(lightning bolt emoji, cat crying emoji)
xoxoxoxo

After the shock of learning David had passed, I began to just
feel grateful that I [had] known his music, art, and creativity.
Grateful that I had appreciated it and immersed myself in it totally.

Becoming a follower of David Bowie happened quite late for
me, regrettably. I grew up in Doncaster, South Yorkshire. The
only knowledge I have of Bowie from an early age is seeing him
in *Labyrinth* and being completed freaked out, but also intrigued
enough to carry on watching. He was different and I couldn't
understand. I wanted to see more. The next time I saw him was
on the 1996 Brit Awards singing "Hallo Spaceboy" with the Pet
Shop Boys. Again I was intrigued, but did not have the impulse
to future explore.

I moved to London at the end of summer 2006. I had accepted

a job at a small design agency. I hadn't finished my degree but I was dead set on moving to London. In my last few weeks of being in Doncaster, I hung out with a friend who had given me hundreds of music files, and within the collection was the two disc *David Bowie at the Beeb*. This became the soundtrack to my first few months in London. I moved there not knowing anyone but my new work colleagues. I was living! Weekends would be spent exploring the city from corner to corner, by foot or bus, my *London A-Z* in hand. Blasting on my iPod mini and in my headphones would be that David Bowie album — I was experiencing Bowie from the beginning — it was wonderful! I ventured far and wide exploring all I could and educating myself on the great man's music. I quickly became a fan of "Janine" and "Karma Man." I lived out west at first and would stroll through Portobello Market whilst listening to "God Knows I'm Good." It was a perfect time. I had no worries: I was free, lived on my own and earned my own money. My only heartache was that my boyfriend was living in the states and I think this made me create my own world with my new interest in Bowie to distract myself. I began to see live bands in Camden with new friends. I learned how people had been influenced by David and my vision of him became richer as my life changed forever over the next few months and years and I became more drawn to his work.

I discovered album after album over the coming years and realized that although he changed his style so much, I could find a place for each in my life. Some days I was in a *Hunky Dory* mood, and others I felt more connected with *Scary Monsters*. I loved this colorful spectrum that was David's music. Although I have obsessively played a lot of his tracks over the years, my all-time favorite is "Heroes." I love this song so much. The video for "Hereos" is so simple, yet beautiful. As I see the artistry I realize that is what makes me a designer. The way the light hits Bowie to make him a silhouette reminds me of an alien at the door of his spaceship, greeting us all. I will always love this video and song; it never gets old and I always come back to it time and time again.

Bowie has left us with a lifetime of musical, artistic talent that we can all enjoy.

FRIENDSHIP AND LOVE
Princess Ramsey, USA

$\mathcal{I}$ WAS A TEENAGER IN the early 1980s. The first David Bowie album I bought was *Scary Monsters*, and it was unlike anything I had ever heard growing up in the south. So dark and raw and enigmatic. The first new album he released after I discovered him was *Let's Dance*, and he was briefly mainstream, almost to my chagrin. I obsessively collected the older albums. Our local record store would save me the best quality used LPs and hold them for me behind the counter. Listening to David Bowie helped me learn at an influential age to be myself. I wasn't an outsider. Bowie made me realize that I wanted to *be*. I wanted to be leading the way, breaking new ground and that is what I have done in my life. His voice touched my soul and informed my personal growth from those days onward.

I did not get to see Bowie play live until 1987; his tours never came near my hometown. I saw the Glass Spider tour at the Meadowlands and was sitting so far from the stage that I had to use my binoculars to see the big screen TVs projecting the show. But the sound was great and the concert was a dream come true for me. It was when I moved to Philadelphia in 1993 that the most enduring influence of David Bowie on my own life really began to come to life. One of the first people I met in Philly was the lovely, kind, generous and all around amazing Patti Bowie. Then the Teenage Wildlifers. Then the BowieNetters. I attended over 30 David Bowie shows in the 1990s and early 2000s. That included a private acoustic set with David and Reeves Gabrels at Sigma Sound for 30 people, where David was so funny we could barely stay in our chairs for laughing. There were too many special moments to recount. I was so lucky to be able to attend all those amazing shows with all those amazing people. And ultimately that is what David Bowie brought to my life: friendship and love. Some of my dearest friends today are among the people I met in those days.

As to David himself, he was always ahead of the times, always creating something completely new, always reflecting our universe from his unique perspective. He was one of the great thinkers of our time and gave us an opus of music, art, word and film to inspire generations to come. He taught us all to be our best, most creative selves, without fear of alienation. It is remarkable that a man dying of cancer spent his last year writing and producing *Lazarus* and recording the most complex and enigmatically beautiful album of his career, *Blackstar*. He was a genuine person, with a rapier wit and keenly intelligent mind. He vanquished the alienation he sought to conquer by bringing so many kindred souls together. In the end he reminded us all to live every moment to the fullest, solely as ourselves. David Bowie certainly did.

PERHAPS I COULD...

Isabelle Flows, UK

A̶T THE BEGINNING, IN 2001, it was my then eight year old sister who showed me *Labyrinth*. When Jareth appeared, I exclaimed "Who the hell is that?" She sighed and looked at me like I was stupid. "It's David Bowie, don't you know anything?" I murmured as I recalled the name written in red on the scary album cover my Dad had in the hallway. I soon forgot about it until I had a dream I was in the goblin battle. I decided to look into him more.

Not many people understood. I was 14, bullied for my choice of music, so of course he quickly became my secret pleasure. When asked what music I liked, I would have to lie.

This went on through to my adulthood. Right up until 2013 and *The Next Day*. I heard the announcement on the radio and screamed in delight. Nothing would stop me now if he were to play live.

Perhaps I could thank him.....perhaps I could have friends who understood....

BowieNet came online again and I could see others who understood. I was not alone! I gave them my hands and it was wonderful.

I had three amazing years. I met many wonderful people,

one who has been a rock in my life. I lived my dream. And yes, I got to scream "thank you" to Bowie at the *Lazarus* premier in December 2015.

David Bowie is…no longer my secret.

RADIO GAGA
RaMoana, USA

$\mathcal{T}$HERE WAS A TIME in late 2000/early 2001 that Bowie disappeared from *BowieNet* and the public. The next photo we saw of him, he had a beard. It was too boring for me with no Bowie on BNet for months, so my friend Diane told me about Live365 and to check out the radio stations there. I tuned into a station and saw anyone could have a station (and it was free then!) and it looked like fun. The next day I started my own station — Transmission Transition — it was alternative and I wanted air time for all these cool bands and songs I liked including Bowie and bands he would mention on BNet too. I included Grandaddy, Neu!, Flaming Lips, Arcade Fire, The Secret Machines, the Dandy Warhols, the list goes on. I found my own bands as well, mostly on *myspace* back then and there was even acid jazz in my playlists! I was busy doing radio work and keeping my rotation list fresh and I occasionally did live shows. So I was not on BNet too much until later in the year, and people would ask me "Where did you go Ramoana?" I said, "If anyone asks, I am away growing a bead (like Bowie)!" So you can thank Bowie's beard for my radio show that has evolved greatly since May 2001 and, for the past ten years, is *The Ramoana Experience on Max Radio*. My three hour show is mostly about Bowie's music as I feel compelled to pay forward all he has given me and is still teaching me! Since his passing, I've learned all sorts of new things, also about his music — like "Heroes" about being a hero to yourself and "Lazarus" is connected to "Starman" — "Starman" is connected to "Somewhere Over the Rainbow," which mentioned a bluebird, like "Lazarus." Although not written by Bowie, the imagery of many "My Death" lyrics show up on both the "Blackstar" and "Lazarus" videos. There is so much more to discover and my strange fascination continues with doing my radio program.

Since I was known on *BowieNet* as doing a Bowie/Bowie-related radio program, I was asked (during the time of the 2nd Tibet House Show) by *BowieNet* to provide the music for the pre-show party. I asked if I could put the latest on there (I was the update demon – always got the latest of whatever Bowie there could be, like Kristeen Young & David Bowie's "Saviour"). I had to make a couple of CDs and FedEx them to New York as I could not attend. I did that and unexpectedly, I was told by Blammo (of *BowieNet*) that he would get something sent to me as a thank you. A year went by and I heard nothing. I asked him about it and he said "working on it." It wasn't my idea, but whatever happened would be ok. Then some months later, a poster arrived at my home.

Upon reading an article this year about Bowie's signature depicting "DRJ" (David Robert Jones) as well as "Bo" and date (the poster does!), I started looking at my poster with signature and had to wonder — not only about the misspelled name "For Ramona" but also the "for" looks like "fu"! Thanks David Bowie-knife Bowie, always the double-edged meaning! I framed it with most of the Reality show tickets I have and it is certainly something I would save in a fire. Bowie's wicked sense of humor is probably what I miss most.

NOTHING MUCH
AT STAKE

Peter Jackson, UK

ᴿECENTLY, ɪɴ ᴛʜᴇ ᴛᴀɴɴᴇᴅ pages of a book, I found evidence of another time. It was a receipt for *The Colin MacInnes Omnibus.* It brings together MacInnes' three London novels, originally published between 1957 and 1960, and it was for the second of these — *Absolute Beginners* — that I was persuaded to buy the omnibus edition. I had never read a word of MacInnes' before, had no real knowledge of the man or his art.

David Bowie's "Absolute Beginners" was released in March 1986, in the run up to the release of Julien Temple's rock musical of the same name. I bought the record on release, the full-length version in heavy gate-fold sleeve. A flyer for merchandise was also included. Its big presentation matched the bigness of the song.

The apparent effortlessness embedded in the song, contributing to the strength of its attraction for me, encouraged a belief at the time that things in my own life would fit together nicely too. Certainly I needed the encouragement: change was coming.

We left university that summer. I had a job to go to, in Leeds, and had found a flat to rent. Initially this period felt more like an ending than the beginning of something new. I missed university;

most of all I missed Jane who I'd shared it with. She had been awarded a British Council grant for a year's post-graduate work, but it was unclear where she would be based. Jane writes to someone who is working down the road at the university in Leeds and is invited to spend a day in the department. By lunchtime she's a member of it and I feel the weariness begin to lift.

As we contemplate our new beginning, I immediately think of the song and David Bowie. "Absolute Beginners" is not a song about starry-eyed lovers starting out for the first time but it's simply about starting out.

I didn't think so at the time, but the small print of my lease worked to our advantage: no co-habiting. Jane found a place almost straight away and I'm only a couple of minutes farther on the other side of the fields. Yet this fledgling time together will prove to be no idyll — we'll need the personal space of our own places as much as their proximity to each other. Work is suffocating, its routines and rigidity barely tolerable. All this talk about the fragility of relationships and the need to be wary; I rail against the world and am not very good company sometimes.

Jane, on the other hand, has intellectual freedoms that I can only dream of and yet she works on her thesis but sees so much loneliness in the most public of places — the library in Headingley. We cling together. In our year in Leeds we don't look much beyond each other emotionally. Naturally, Bowie is caught up in all this too. My favorites of his songs remain embedded in past times, but Bowie is always moving forward.

While I listened to Bowie, Jane worked on the final part of her thesis and together we prepared for the next step. We began to look beyond Leeds. Jane passes her degree. By way of celebration, we jump in the car and go see Bowie.

The Glass Spider Tour of 1987 was, up until that point, his most ambitious, expensive and extensive tour. We saw him emerge from the Glass Spider stage set in Manchester, at the Maine Road

Stadium on 14 July. The spider is above and all around, pulsing and glowing, and the stage is already crowded and stays that way. Bowie's voice cuts strong and he looks great in his red suit, blond hair bouncing. And then it's into "Absolute Beginners." It's little more than a year since we first heard it, but already it seems timeless.

The show is long, over two hours. He sings a fantastic version of "Time," still singing as he abseils down and unbuckles himself on the stage. The entire audience is singing too, some overcome with emotion. A girl near us is sobbing hysterically, strands of hair stuck to her face, yet singing at the same time.

It's Bowie and not on his weakest night. At the end of the show, as people drift towards the exits, many take a last look back at the stage set, the spider still pulsing with light. No one has the slightest notion this will be the last they'll see David Bowie performing in this way.

Back in Leeds we have to move on too. I think of Jane packing her things away and feel grateful for the year we've had, happy too that Bowie has played such a big part in it — as he always does — as he always will. The next morning we combine our belongings and the sun is shining as we clamber into the cab, laughing together, and knowing that we are not absolute beginners any more.

BERLIN WAS WHERE WE SHOULD HAVE BEEN

Charlie Raven, UK

$\mathscr{B}$ERLIN WAS ALWAYS JUST over there, an idea hanging in the air. In the winter of 1976 going into 1977, I was stranded on a brutal emotional flat line.

The summer of 1976 had been spent on the river. There was a boat, a little rowing boat, and we loved it. All that hot dry summer long, quietly dipping the oars, watching rafts of ladybirds float past. We spoke about everything under the sun. We were high on each other's company. Anything was possible because we were just turning 18.

I didn't know we were in love, I didn't see that one coming. I just knew that all I wanted to do was be with her and to talk to her and to write to her and that seemed normal. What best friends always do. We were scheduled to part. She was going to university; I was going to start my first job. It hung over us, this terrible parting. Although we said we'd write and always be friends, I knew that she would be seduced by new friends, find a boyfriend, because that's the fate of girls. That's the real world.

I know when we first talked it was actually about being in love with David Bowie. I remember standing in the school corridor and there she was actually holding the newly purchased LP of *Aladdin Sane* under her arm. That extraordinarily disturbing image of the starved face and the lightning flash caused various reactions among the other girls, which is why this girl was displaying it in the first place — so that the David Cassidy girls would exhibit exaggerated disdain or repulsion.

I plucked up courage and I said shyly, "I really like Bowie" and the girl warmed and smiled and said with sudden enthusiasm, "They wouldn't show the video for "John, I'm Only Dancing" on *Top of the Pops*! Can you believe that?"

"Really?" I said politely, not knowing anything about this.

"They just don't get it." Continued the girl. "They're all scared of him. And this LP means *a lad insane*, get it? Aladdin, a lad insane. Clever, he is."

I agreed and felt a little stronger and braver on behalf of the lad insane with the lightning bolt streaking across his face, right there in the corridor waiting to go into the German lesson. And the girl and I became firm friends.

Over the next couple of years we'd go round to each other's house and talk about Bowie all the time: do you love him because he is a man or because he is not like a man? And where will you find a real man like that? So do you want a girl to be your boyfriend or a boy to be your girlfriend? And we'd laugh, not sure if we were boys or girls.

Bowie was secretly a cipher for how that uncontrollable, unpredictable thing called sex might turn out to be something other than straight, submissive, humiliating and baby bearing. And Bowie didn't hide. He handed his attackers all the ammunition they needed, peeling off layers to reveal softness, showing how the separate parts of his identity — biological sex, gender identity, sexuality — was split at the root and looped back and grew away again in unlikely directions.

So finally there was a hesitant conversation in her bedroom

where I said that I loved her and she said that she loved me, knowing it didn't mean a thing to say that because we were two girls and girls had to get boyfriends and marry and have babies. Girls might love other girls because even old Jane Eyre loved her friend who died of consumption, and that was the acceptable kind of love that I almost thought I meant. But I didn't really, because there was the awareness that people of the same sex could and did love each other. At the same time, there was no doubt in my mind that those people were damaged and sad. If they could sometimes be scintillating and gorgeous, like David Bowie, if that only applied to me…

My sensitive internal self-image was synchronized to Bowie's in a subtle and completely unconscious way: his becoming a dog on the cover of *Diamond Dogs*, for example, and my own becoming a piece of teenage not-very-wild life shadowed each other. There was a part of me that knew by now that I really didn't want to grow up to be one of those women on the cover of Roxy Music or an awful bikini-clad Bond girl. What would I become if I didn't grow up to be a woman then? A hybrid creature, a monster, one of the "Strangest Living Curiosities"? There seemed not a lot of future in that. So when I felt brave enough to say that I loved my friend, it did not imply that we would or could express our love in any physical way.

And one particular day in the summer of '76, we took a book of poems to the river and read aloud to each other and a beautiful liquid understanding flowed between us. We crept a little way into a grove of trees and then laid down side by side in the sun; and I gradually felt warm and physically attracted by her presence. But I didn't know what should come of that and anyway we were interrupted. And it took on a shadowy tone, a secret thing that could never bear fruit and could never be mentioned. It was one of those loves that dares not speak its name.

We spent a lot of time in my room playing "Station to Station" that summer, staring through the ceiling or the walls, trying to catch every glistening, freezing note:

> *"It's not the side effects of the cocaine — I'm thinking that it must be love"*

And 1976 had been all about that — wrongness and thinking that it must be love. Anyway, Bowie couldn't stop time for us. It happened. The parting. And the world of work took me and the world of university took her. At first we wrote almost continuously. I always had a letter on the go. There was always a letter waiting to be read, usually copious pages of thick green ink.

On a cold November weekend, she came and stayed and the next thing happened, the next station: we made love. We walked awkwardly round the park early the next day, a Sunday morning, and in my head I could hear Lou Reed singing, "Sunday morning, And I'm falling..."

Reed's blighted, beautiful song and the streets we'd crossed that Sunday morning; and I could sense that because we had made love, because we had become lovers, that she would begin to move away now. The distance was already there between us.

Sure enough, the weeks passed by and letters came more infrequently. Finally came a letter which mentioned a boy and a relationship. There was no formal ending of what we had. It was just shunted into a siding and left to fall apart. The winter passed.

In the Spring of 1977 I devoted myself instead to the *New Musical Express* and *Melody Maker* and David Bowie and Iggy Pop. I listened continually to *Low* and *The Idiot*. I became obsessed with the fact that Bowie and Iggy were now living in Berlin together. Of course I didn't consciously know anything about it at the time, but our ghosts had moved to Berlin along with them – to inhabit the bodies of two rock stars, kick their cocaine and smack habits and write the best music of a generation. But there we were.

In one imaginary Berlin, there were the two damaged individuals and they looked good but felt bad. In another, dying of starvation and drugs and drink one is brought food and blankets by the other and finally, wearing thick frayed coats in the snow they would walk quietly together. People knew there was something special between them, but nobody ever said anything about it.

And that was us, you see. That was what it was like when we were in our imaginary Berlin. When I needed a place to put that ramshackle mess of first love, Bowie held onto it and turned it into "Heroes."

MAKEUP AND FEATHER BOAS AND SEQUINS

Christina Prass, USA

*M*y first memory of David is when I was sitting in the back of my Dad's car. I was age six. I would take out the CD insert for *Ziggy Stardust and the Spiders from Mars* and sing my heart out, especially to "Starman." I also loved looking at the picture of this man in makeup and feather boas and sequins. It was an instant love affair.

Fast forward nine years. I was completely obsessed. All the albums, enough shirts to wear a different one for nearly two weeks. Kids I didn't even know at school knew I was "the Bowie girl." August 2002 was the first time I got to see Bowie perform live when my dad got tickets to the Area 2 tour. But it wasn't just any show; it was the infamous Jones Beach, NY show. A storm had started to roll in and by the time David got on stage it was pouring. Lightning was crashing down all around this stage on the water. Of course, this caused the show to be cut short for safety reasons, but not before the most rousing, memorable rendition of "Heroes" I ever heard. The audience was wild and David seemed as though he could not have cared less about the weather. This left an impression on me.

The second time I saw Bowie was just a few months later at an intimate show at the Beacon Theater for his NY Marathon Tour for *Heathen*. This time (unbeknownst to my mother) my father pumped out quite a bit of money to score us fourth row end seats. It was a fantastic night. Everyone would run down the aisle to the stage to touch his hand, but I was too shy; something, of course, that I regret now. During "Fame" he did point and smile right at me during the "What's your name?" part!

My next show was the following year, back at Jones Beach. I was a member of *BowieNet* by then and we organized a barbecue on the beach before the show. There were a lot of great memories from that and it was so wonderful to meet other Bowie fans. I believe the farthest fan had come from Germany. I had brought a small cardboard cutout of Bowie that a record store let me take and we had a lot of fun including him in the festivities. We all signed a giant banner and a beach ball and somewhere there is a picture of Bowie holding the beach ball.

My final time seeing David was December 2003 at Madison Square Garden. This time I was the one that shelled out the money (ALL of my confirmation money, much to my mother's displeasure) and we had 8th row floor seats. It was another fantastic show, the band was so relaxed and everyone seemed to be having a really great time. A lot of banter and dorky jokes and stories came from David. I watch the Reality DVD often these days and it always brings me to tears since that was the "David" I knew. I'm forever grateful to have these memories and that I had the chance to see him.

After Bowie's death I received so many texts, messages and phone calls from people checking in to see if I was ok and offering condolences. Everyone knew what he meant to me. My sister said it was as though we had lost a family member. I would not have survived some of my darkest days without Bowie, as so many hours were spent watching his videos over and over to escape the real world. I would not be the person I am today if it hadn't been for David Bowie, nor would I have had the courage to be myself. He opened my mind and my heart. When he died a piece of my soul left with him and although I'll never stop missing him, I wouldn't change a thing.

I FOUND BOWIE, THEN I FOUND ME

Caroline Thompson, UK

A Bowie story begun by Craig Thompson and
concluded by Caroline Thompson.

$\mathcal{M}$Y NAME IS NOW Caroline Thompson, but once upon a time I was Craig Thompson crane driver and demolition man. I discovered Bowie in 1972 when I heard "Starman" on the radio. At the time, I was working for a company that was involved in slum clearance and demolition around South London and mainly Battersea. I always took my portable transistor radio to work with me; it was a little Russian made radio called a Sokol, it had a little earpiece which I wore under my ear defenders. It was an interesting time in my life. I recall having to stop one afternoon for some filming right where I was working. It was a scene for a British comedy film called *Ooh You Are Awful* starring comedian Dick Emery.

One day I heard "Starman" on my radio. I hadn't heard anything like this before and I thought it was one of the most beautiful songs I'd ever come across. I heard "Starman" several times that week on various radio stations. I never did see the TV appearance where Bowie put his arm around Mick Ronson that's now infamous, but all the same I was drawn to Bowie. I went and bought whatever Bowie I could find. I bought his first four albums and thought *The Rise and Fall of Ziggy Stardust and the Spiders From Mars* was just the most perfect record. It was just an awesome album, idea, set of ideas, values, predictions and it was prophetic in many ways as it told the story of an outsider and how the outsider fits and will come to fit even more as the future that we make unfolds.

I always read the bit about "I had to break up the band" as "I've lit the blue paper, now my work is done, it's up to you, the future is yours so take it." I was pretty obsessed with Bowie and what he stood for and I had an epiphany. I suddenly found my confidence and I found honesty. I wasn't happy and I'd been living a lie. I wasn't happy and I knew why. I had always felt female in a male body. I told myself to stop denying the truth. I told my mum and dad, they were incredibly supportive and I think inside they knew I was different. I had always fancied boys but not in a same sex way.

It's hard to explain, but Bowie showed me the way. I felt great for the first time in my life, really great. Just coming out to myself and my parents was such a relief. I began seeking medical help and treatment. It's actually not much different from today, excuse the pun, but they had it sewn up pretty much in those days too.

The day Bowie retired as Ziggy Stardust was the day I became Caroline Thompson, 3 July 1973. For me the album was about peace and love. I found peace and I found love as Caroline Thompson. I kept up with Bowie over the years and last saw him live on the Reality tour in Dublin. I will never forget those early days and how brave Bowie was. He asked us to be ourselves whatever we were. When I think of all his characters and creations, I think of "Changes" and how Bowie would say "if you're not happy then change things." Well I did.

Thank you, David.

IT HAPPENED ONE DAY

YOUR CAR IS OUTSIDE
Patti Brett, USA

$\mathcal{M}$Y FRIENDS AND I were following the Station to Station tour in 1976, traveling along the East Coast and into New England. We were friendly with Carlos Alomar who had given us a list of hotels that the band would be staying at. Arriving at the Americana Hotel in Rochester, New York we checked in shortly after the band had arrived.

When we got to our rooms, we looked in the phone book for a place to do laundry. As we were unfamiliar with the town, we were not sure what places were close by. I jotted down a few addresses and we went back down to the lobby to ask for help in finding a place that was relatively close.

Dressed in Bowie t-shirts, we asked the clerk at the front desk if he knew where the closest laundromat was. He replied, "It doesn't matter, we have a car outside for you that will take you wherever you'd like to go!"

He thought we were with the band! That explained why they gave us rooms on the same floor as David!

When we left town the next morning headed to the next concert stop, we heard on the radio that David had been arrested! [Bowie was arrested at the hotel in Rochester on charges of marijuana possession. The charges were later dismissed. *Ed.*]

EAVESDROPPING
ON BOWIE

Chris Hughes, UK

On 1988 I'd already graduated from university and was living in a flatshare in Chelsea, London SW3 with some university friends.

One night I was coming home late — probably around 1 or 2 am — and as I walked up Draycott Avenue, I saw two couples standing by a black cab which had pulled over for them. They seemed to be saying goodbye to each other, then one of the couples got into the taxi and it drove off, while the other couple walked hand-in-hand along the pavement towards me.

The woman was strikingly attractive with pale skin, a mass of dark hair and scarlet lips. The man seemed more ordinary looking with relatively short hair, a neat light brown beard and glasses. Only when they were almost in front of me did I realize that the man was David Bowie! When he suddenly laughed at something the woman had said, and in the glare of the bright streetlights, I spotted the distinctively uneven Bowie teeth and then the mismatched eyes behind the glasses.

I was so stunned that, in the words of Burt Bacharach, I *"walked on by!"*

But this was David Bowie! Right there on the pavement, just a few paces from my front door in Denyer Street! I couldn't miss the opportunity to speak to the man whose music had completely defined my adolescent years, so I quickly turned and headed after him. While I tried to figure out what to say to him, I kept a respectful distance — not wishing him to fear that I was another Mark Chapman. I was fascinated by the fragments of conversation that I was able to overhear — he seemed to be describing the television puppet shows of Gerry Anderson while the woman shrieked with laughter. I heard him tell her how "Pete and Dud" (Peter Cook and Dudley Moore) had parodied the awkward, lumbering gait of the "Thunderbirds" puppets to great comic effect, and then I heard Bowie imitate the melodramatic voiceover at the start of "Stingray": "STAND BY FOR ACTION!" With his voice he reproduced the frantic drumming which followed this announcement during that opening sequence — and then the next voiceover: "Anything can happen in the next half hour!" Then I heard him say "And they had this mermaid who was mute! Oh man, she was really something — she looked like Brigitte Bardot with dark hair." I realized he was describing the puppet character "Marina" from "Stingray." Just as I hoped that Bowie was about to croon a verse or two of her theme tune "Aqua Marina," he spotted a black cab, hailed it and was gone before I could approach him.

So near, but yet so far.

BOWIE SLEPT IN MY BED

Chris Buxbaum, UK

$\mathcal{M}$Y FIRST APARTMENT WAS a semi coldwater flat above my Dad's transport café "The Go To It Café" in Park Royal, London. The upstairs had not been lived in for 10 years, but I took two of the rooms and cleaned and decorated them. The rest of the place was dusty and kind of spooky.

Downstairs the Café was giant and busy. It had been used once or twice as a film location due to its proximity to BBC's Shepherds Bush Studio. Imagine my shock when my dad said they were going to shoot a movie (*The Hunger*) there and, oh by the way, *David Bowie* is in it! I did not believe him and was sure he was pulling my leg, but it really was true.

With great difficulty, I was able to get the day off from work, still not sure if Bowie was actually going to be in the scene they were shooting that day. I had been a devoted fan for ten years at this point and my nerves were totally shot. The day before the crew had blacked out all the windows in the café and parked two yellow NYC cabs outside. They turned one half of the inside of the café into a real American diner complete with flickering neon signs and chrome counters.

The crew arrived early the next day and Bowie was there in his limo driven, if memory serves me, by his chauffeur from *The*

Man Who Fell To Earth. About an hour later a production assistant asked my Dad if Bowie could use the flat upstairs as his trailer had not showed up. My Dad said, "ask my son as it's his place." How could I say no? It doesn't bear thinking about…David Bowie in my crappy flat above a greasy spoon in a crappy part of London. What were the chances?

My plan was simple; after I was introduced I was going to stay out of the way all day until he was finished working and then try and get some pictures and maybe get an album or two signed. I figured if I was respectful and didn't act like a rabid fan, I would get better results. It wasn't easy. The place was next to Park Royal Hospital and while they were setting up the shot, loads of nurses came over to oogle and chat. He signed tons of autographs and was gracious and funny with everyone. I hung back, keeping to my plan.

The way it was set up, I could see the shoot through an interior archway from about 4 feet away. They shot the 2 minute scene numerous times from 7 am until 7 pm. The scene which was never in the final movie, takes place while Bowie's hunger is increasing but before he has started to age. A young punky girl in a vinyl raincoat, possibly a hooker and played by Zoe Wanamaker, is sitting in a booth. Bowie joins her and makes polite conversation and buys her a hamburger. He says "You should get away from me while you can." She doesn't understand. The burger comes and she takes one bite. (This was quite amusing because she did this about 20 times and was really a vegetarian. She seemed to get greener by the take.) She starts to shake the ketchup. It accidentally goes all over her fetching vinyl attire looking like blood dripping down. Bowie's eyes flicker, his breathing quickens and he licks his lips. End of scene.

During the afternoon break, Bowie says he is knackered (he does look tired and possibly a little hungover) and can he take a nap in my bed? How could I refuse? The bedroom was just a mattress on a floor of Japanese straw mats with big Kanji painted on the walls. On my bedside table was a ZG (Zeitgeist) magazine, an intellectual art mag. This specific issue was about S&M/Fetishism in art and he read it for half an hour before taking a short nap. When he awoke they reapplied his make-up at a makeshift movie star mirror they installed in my living room. I offered him some wine which he drank straight from the bottle. I took his picture with the wine which he wasn't very happy about. He said, "We will take some later, I promise."

The workday wound to a close and I had all my albums lined up expectantly. *Space Oddity* through *Scary Monsters* plus tons of bootlegs. He came up and we took a few pictures. He looked through all my albums by other artists and asked me what I though was cool and what clubs were happening. I had DJ'd at the Blitz as a cover for Rusty Egan and was currently DJing at a night club called The Great Wall playing only Asian music. He was very interested in that. He pulled out my original 45 of "The Prettiest Star" and said he didn't even have a copy himself. He played it and commented on how amazing he thought Marc Bolan's guitar solo was. After about an hour he went downstairs and asked his driver to wait a little longer. I couldn't believe it.

We chatted more about Bolan. He talked about how Burroughs had told him to stop dressing outrageously. He said it was more subversive for an artist to blend into the background. He signed all the albums except for the boots.

He took my original *Space Oddity* and made notations on George Underwood's painting on the back pointing out who the Guru was and that the girl was Hermione. I still have it to this day. He showed me a picture of him and Zowie on the ski slopes and met my sister and my girlfriend who arrived later.

David Bowie finally left me with a picture that said, "To Chris, Thanks for the use of your Gaff (and the sounds). Bowie 82"

WAITING FOR DAVID — LEIPZIG 1997

Simone Metge, Germany

I FELL IN LOVE WITH David the first time I saw him live on June 7, 1997 at the Go Bang festival in Lubeck. He came on stage in his white clothes, looking like an angel, singing "Quicksand" and I was hooked. I became totally addicted then — even though I had liked his music generally over the previous few years. I was able to see two more concerts within a month, but unfortunately they were also at festivals.

At the second concert, in Leipzig, I overheard a conversation of a few girls who talked about friends who were still waiting for David at his hotel. It was the first time I had ever heard of that possibility and I wouldn't have thought of it myself. After the show I went to the hotel and naively asked if he was staying there. The receptionist actually sent me to a different hotel where they responded "no comment" to my question.

It didn't matter; I knew which hotel the girls had mentioned, so the next morning I went again and saw several people waiting. I hung out as well. While waiting a lady showed me concert photos she had taken. I didn't exchange names with any of these people,

but later found out I had already met some friends back then for
the first time.

We waited for quite a while. Many people walked by as it was
Protestant *Kirchentag*. To anyone who asked who we were waiting
for we told them the name of a German politician so no one else
stopped to wait with us.

After a while, David finally came out. I started to scream a
little squeal but managed to stop as I noticed everyone else was
quiet. I was embarrassed. Unfortunately, David didn't stop at all
but climbed into his bus. I was really disappointed, as I would
have loved to have gotten his autograph. I went home crying as I
thought this would never happen to me again. Little did I know
my future would provide many more occasions to see David.

I WAS SUPPOSED TO SEE HILDA OGDEN[1]...BUT SAW DAVID BOWIE INSTEAD

Tracey Chorlton, UK

⌀s a kid I was obsessed with the TV show *Coronation Street*, and not only did I watch every episode but I collected what little memorabilia was available then. Usually there were articles in newspapers and magazines and I had tea mugs and calendars. At the time, my greatest ambition was to meet the stars of Coronation Street. I considered then, and still do, the 1970s to be the golden years for *Coronation Street*; it was full of stars and great female characters battling on in a man's world. My Nan said I should write to *Jim'll Fix It* to see if I could get to meet the cast of *Coronation Street*.

I wrote my letter and to my amazement I actually got a reply. I wasn't going to be on the TV show, but I was going to be given a tour of the Granada Studios TV set in late August. The big day came and my older brother drove me to Manchester. We were met by a nice lady named Paula who took us to a canteen and said we could have food for free and that sometimes the cast popped in.

---

[1] A character in the BBC Television series *Coronation Street*.

We had only been in the canteen a matter of minutes when actress Helen Worth came in for tea. I was so impressed and nervous at the same time. Paula came back to sit with us and mentioned there were some scenes being filmed and shortly we would be walked around the set, but she couldn't guarantee that we'd meet anyone in particular. I was keeping my fingers crossed in the hope that I would meet Hilda... please, please please! It was quite a while before Paula came back and informed us that there had been an accident on set and we could not visit today. I was gutted, so gutted. She told us to stay put and she would see what she could do to make up for it.

When Paula returned she asked if we'd like to watch Marc Bolan's TV show as they were filming the last show in the series. I wasn't bothered, but my brother was ecstatic at the prospect of seeing Marc Bolan! We were taken to another studio and were seated in the audience. It wasn't a huge studio, but you could see it was set up for several bands. Filming began and took a few hours.

I didn't really know who was who, but my brother knew Generation X, and I really liked Eddie and the Hot Rods as they performed "Anything You Wanna Do." There were some dancers that were very good.

David Bowie came on to sing "Heroes" and although I was aware of Bowie (you couldn't not be aware of him in the 1970s) I was not a fan, but something about him just drew me in. I became a fan that instant — his posture, his singing, his voice, his looks; I thought this was the most beautiful man I'd ever seen. The duet with Bolan at the end is now legendary. Just as they were really getting into it, the floor director called time and that was that.

Bolan died not long after, and it was weird seeing the show air in late September on a black and white TV. I never did get to meet Hilda Ogden, but I did see Bowie a few times in concert. David

Bowie and Jean Alexandra (Hilda Ogden) both died in 2016 and it is odd how they are connected in my memory.

I was able to see Bowie and Bolan purely by accident, but I will always cherish that day. I wish we had smart phones back then so I could have taken a picture.

THE AUTOGRAPH
IS IN THE MAIL
Marla Kanevsky, USA

$\mathcal{O}$VER THE YEARS I have had the pleasure and complete honor
to have had many encounters with David Bowie. I have been a
devotee since 1973; I am from Philadelphia and have seen David
in Philly at every show except his first one. I also saw various
concerts in several cities throughout the USA. I was definitely in
the right place at the right time during the period David was in
Philly recording *Young Americans* at Sigma Sound Studios (1974). I
had stars in my eyes and stardust (glitter) in my hair as one of the
Sigma Kids who were graciously invited by David into the studio
late one night to have a listening party with him, the fabulous
musicians, wonderful photographer Dagmar and others. David
Bowie was interested in our opinions on the newest musical road
he was on. It was incredible. But this story is not about Sigma.

Over the years, my son Zane was able to meet David on
several occasions. The first time was in 1995, when David toured
with Nine Inch Nails. We were given backstage passes by the
incomparable Carlos Alomar and after the show we had a meet
and greet with members of the band. This was the first time Zane
met David — Zane was seven at the time. He knew he was in the

presence of a very special person and had been a fan since birth. Zane said to David, "My Mom got my name from one of your songs!" David, without skipping a beat, got down on his knee to Zane's level and said "I know!" and then sang a few lines from "All the Madmen" — "*Zane, Zane, Zane...*"

Going further back in time, however, in 1990 David was in town for the Sound and Vision Tour. At this time, Zane was three. My friends and I found out where David was staying — at the Four Seasons in Philadelphia —- and we hung outside. Most of the time we got rooms ourselves. For some reason, I got the idea to write a letter to David, reminding him that I was a "Sigma Kid." I asked him (never believing it would happen) to sign an autograph for Zane and send it back to me. I even enclosed a self-addressed stamped envelope. My wonderful friend Jimmy, who was an employee of the hotel, did an amazing favor for me. He slipped the note under David's hotel room door! Well, I thought. That was that.

One week later while checking my mail, I see the self-addressed stamped envelope! And, yes, inside was an autograph for Zane! This reinforces what we all know. David was a kind man who I truly believe had a special place in his heart for children.

Even though we did not meet with David in person during this particular experience, I think this still may be my favorite.

Of course there was the time in 1997, but that's another story...

BOWIE MYTHS

Anonymous, UK

 $\mathcal{O}$ N OCTOBER 2010, IT was widely reported that the legendary international literary agent Andrew Wylie was touting a rather special book around that year's Frankfurt Book Fair. David Bowie was writing an unconventional autobiography that would be told by way of a catalogue of objects which had been particularly significant in his life and career. The book was to be called *BOWIE: OBJECT*. The initial buzz surrounding such an exciting prospect, coupled with the fact that the book subsequently failed to materialize, inspired me to create a hoax in which it would be suggested that a section of the manuscript of the book had been leaked online.

First I set up a website (*BowieMyths*), then a co-conspirator and I wrote a stack of posts (plus fictional below-the-line comments) going back months in order to create the impression that *BowieMyths* had had a life of its own for some time and was not put together solely to host the leaked manuscript.

Having been a huge fan of David Bowie for more than thirty years, I'd read dozens of interviews with Bowie and articles that he'd written for publication. But it was the preface to Mick Rock's book *Moonage Daydream* which was truly a (velvet) goldmine for the creation of the fake *BOWIE: OBJECT* text, being so incredibly simple to pastiche. As an autodidact, David Bowie was always keen to display the breadth of his references, but he also used self-deprecating wit if he ever sensed himself veering into pretentiousness. I've heard entertainers who do vocal impersonations say that once you find the correct words and phrases that your subject would use, all the idiosyncratic inflections and rhythms of speech follow naturally. The same is also true of writing. As I drafted the fake extract of *BOWIE: OBJECT*, I knew I had the right words when I could hear his voice speaking the text as it appeared on the screen.

Once the fake extract was published on *BowieMyths* under the breathless banner headline "*BOWIE: OBJECT*— EXCLUSIVE PREVIEW!" the response was phenomenal. News outlets all over the world fell for it hook, line and sinker and within days the "exclusive preview" had been quoted in the press from Singapore to Sydney to San Francisco. Suddenly real fans were visiting the site and posting real messages! In one three-day period, we received in excess of 148,000 unique visitors — up from barely double figures in previous days. Of course scams like this can be easily exposed and when Bowie's official Facebook page dismissed the whole thing as a hoax, most people accepted that they'd been duped and the fun was over (although oddly, one fan who posted obsessively in various David Bowie fan forums, categorically refused to accept that it was a hoax and continues to insist that "the person who wrote it must have seen Bowie's manuscript" even after I later amended the wording of the *BowieMyths* article to make it absolutely clear that I'd made it all up!)

But — this book you are reading is called *My Bowie Story*, so how does David Bowie himself fit in?

In the height of the media feeding frenzy about the story, I received a direct message to my Administrator account which just said "ho, ho, ho. db." The cynic in me assumed that someone was now setting out to hoax the hoaxer, so I replied, "Adam Buxton,

I presume?" (Adam Buxton is the British writer and comedian whose obsession with David Bowie manifested itself in the hilarious series of "Cobbler Bob" videos on YouTube). A response pinged back literally within seconds: "is there a number I can reach you at right now? db." Not for one second imagining this would be David Bowie, I played along, quite excited at the thought that it might be Adam Buxton. Ten minutes after emailing my number, my phone rang. The screen showed no caller information, only "unavailable."

Me: Hello...who's this?

Him: Why, it's Cobbler Bob, of course.

Me: Mr. Buxton, it's an honour.

Him: Oh dear, I'm not sure that me pretending to be Adam Buxton is going to cause quite the same kind of international incident as you pretending to be me.

The voice did rather sound like David Bowie.

Me: That's not bad, Adam. You sound more like him when you speak. But you use too much vibrato when you start singing.

Him: Oh, really? Thank you very much, I'll bear that in mind.....

Then he laughed. And the laugh sent shivers up my spine. The laugh was indisputably genuine. Full-throated, but dried out and roughened by decades of nicotine addiction. A laugh that every fan has heard thousands of times watching and re-watching interviews.

Bowie said it was fascinating that I'd recognized his laugh but not his voice. I said I felt a bit embarrassed about the hoax which I hoped he realized was affectionate (he did) and not intended to be a nasty piss-take. He joked that there was no need for him to do his own book now because it could never be quite as "quintessentially

Bowie-esque" (his phrase) as the piece I'd written. He talked a bit about that "Nat Tate" hoax he had perpetrated with William Boyd and he said he wanted to call me because he knew how much fun I must have had putting together *BowieMyths* because he said that he and William Boyd had enjoyed the preparation of "Nat Tate" almost more than the execution. He said his favourite part of the *BowieMyths* website was the thread which claimed to have found sheet music of old songs which had the same titles as Bowie compositions – in reality, they'd all been Photoshopped, of course.

> Him: "The Heart's Filthy Lesson" by the Beverley Sisters
>   — that one killed me! The f★★★ing Beverley Sisters!

He roared with laughter.

I asked if he was going to record or tour again. He told me he had no inclination to make music any more (which I now know was untrue as it's since become clear that he was secretly working on *The Next Day* at the time). He said he was done with the industry, that he had nothing left to give, that he was able to live fairly anonymously in New York and was able to take his daughter to the zoo and just generally enjoy the kind of simple family life he'd missed out on with his son.

> Me: Well if you do ever decide to tour again, can I put in an
>   early request for three songs you've never played live?
> Him: And which songs would they be?
> Me: "Shadow Man", "Win" and "We Are The Dead".
> Him: You know we actually rehearsed "Win" for the last
>   tour, but I don't know…all the songs from the "Young
>   Americans" album, apart from "Fame", all those songs
>   really need a different kind of band…

The conversation lasted no longer than ten or fifteen minutes, but I was so wrong-footed by the whole surreal experience that I only thought of all the things I really wanted to ask him after the call had ended.

And if Adam Buxton or anyone else wants to come forward and try to persuade me it was really them who spoke to me that day, they'll first need to tell me approximately what time of day the call took place (UK time) and what we said about something that Bowie's daughter and my niece have in common. If you can't tell me those details, then don't even try it!

In any case, I'd know that laugh anywhere.

WE ALL SANG IN UNISON
Bella Aptekar, USA

$\mathcal{I}$ WAS BORN INTO THE David Bowie universe decades after his heyday. As a teenager, it didn't take long for music to inhabit me, my life, and my soul. What a gift it was for Bowie's music to find me at my most uncertain. Inhabiting identities was what he did and seemed to encourage. What better time to embrace such an ideology than during my inscrutable adolescence? He served as a guide, a parent of intellectual rebellion and creative mischief.

For a Holmdel, New Jersey stop on The Reality Tour, I brought a poster sign with me to catch his attention. I was a virginal nineteen year old, clamoring to fit in with the elders who had lived through each and every Bowie incarnation and had grown up in a world where rock and roll was scandalous.

"When you rock n' roll with me, no one else I'd rather be. Thank you for coming back!" I wrote on the sign. During the low key guitar jam in "Sister Midnight," he sauntered over, strumming, and read it. Oh, to have the sun shine on you for even a second! My friend punched me in the arm when David threw a wink my way. A wink. A tangible moment from an ineffable feeling.

I remember looking back behind me that night. Four thousand people joyfully shouted *"Wham, Bam, Thank You Ma'am!"* The way I imagine we all do by ourselves in the car or at home when a Bowie song comes on the radio. Except on this night, and on the nights following his death, we all sang in unison. A secret club having a rare meeting, exchanging secret handshakes. And when the leader exited, we remained.

If life were a movie, my closing credits would play over a scene from my twentieth birthday; drunk and happy, my friends and I stumbled home harmonizing a tune I taught them from "Memory of a Free Festival" — "*The sun machine is coming down, and we're gonna have a party. Oh, oh, oh!*"

I WROTE TO BOWIE AND BOWIE WROTE BACK

Eric Isaacson, Canada

On 1980, I was fortunate enough to go to New York City and see David Bowie in *The Elephant Man*. Not only was his performance masterful and mesmerizing, it was also believable and heartfelt.

The following year I was to spend a semester in Israel, on a Dawson College program, working and studying on a kibbutz. Being an extreme David Bowie fanatic, I worried that I would miss any tour he might do in 1981. To ease my mind, I took a chance and wrote a letter to him at the Booth Theatre, where the play took place. I asked if he would be out on tour during the months I would be away. I never really expected a response. Two weeks later, to my complete surprise and amazement, I received a hand-written letter signed by him. He said that he had no plans to tour during the dates I mentioned and that I should have a "wonderful and interesting" time. I will never forget the euphoria I experienced at that moment. That he took time from his busy schedule to write meant the world to me.

I've been enthralled and captivated by his talent and creations for over forty years; and though his time here on earth has come to an end, I will continue to cherish his brilliant legacy. I look up to the stars and thank the heavens there was David Bowie.

A PREMIER AND A HELLO
Steve Lock, UK

$\mathcal{H}$AVING BEEN A FAN since 1972 when I was 11 years old, and having just seen David Bowie live in concert, it was the 14th of February 1979 that friends and I decided to travel to see the world premiere of *Just a Gigolo*. It was showing at the Prince Charles cinema in Leicester Square, London and we had hopes of catching a glimpse of our hero.

We arrived early in the morning to the venue and made inquiries if we were at the correct cinema. We also asked if David would make an appearance. Fortunately, one of the film promoters was there arranging points of display and overheard our inquisitive questions. Impressed by the fact that we had travelled 150 miles to simply catch a glimpse of David, she gave me her business card and told me to give her a call later that day. She was going to try and get us some promotional material. After what seemed a lifetime of waiting, I telephoned her late in the afternoon and she instructed me to come on my own to her offices in Dean Street, London.

Without hesitation, I was on my way. I remember clearly how frantic everyone was when I entered the building, but very impressed by our newly found friend and contact, Jacki Simons. She gave me three complimentary tickets for the premier.

Seeing David enter the cinema that evening and greet

everyone from the upstairs balcony was unforgettable. After the film had finished, while we were in the front foyer of the cinema, I approached Jacki Simons to thank her for her kindness. She asked me if I would like to meet David. I stood there shocked, but eagerly said "yes." She took me to the bottom of the stairway to gain access, but we were declined for the simple reason of not being appropriately dressed. It was a black suit and tie event upstairs.

Disappointed, we waited in the foyer for what seemed an eternity but I managed to get a "hello" from David as he left.

DUBLIN 1999
Simone Metge, Germany

$\mathcal{A}$FTER SEEING DAVID AT several festivals in 1997, I didn't see him again until 1999. By then I had made several friends who were fans of his as well, I had signed up for *BowieNet*, and I planned on going to Gisborne where he was supposed to play a Millennium Concert. After finding that the concert wouldn't happen after all, I eagerly waited for his next album (*Hours*) and followed him on his mini tour around Europe.

First there was the TV show, *TFI Friday*, then NetAid and then we flew to Dublin to see him perform at the tiny HQ Club. There was absolutely no gap between the stage and audience and the stage was really low. Placebo was playing as his support, and I was standing in the front row nearly getting hit by a guitar due to the stage being right at my feet! What a wonderful experience this was after the festivals.

When David came on stage a few people even managed to shake his hand or give him flowers. I had considered doing this too as I carried a self-made marzipan rose with me for days, but decided to wait for a better moment.

After the concert, four or five of us went to his hotel to wait for him. David was very sweet. He shook my hand and I gave him the marzipan rose (but sadly forgot to mention that I made it myself). I asked him to sign a photo I took of him at my second concert in Leipzig. He did, and signed it exactly the way I hoped he would: with a silver pen and dedicated to me, "For Simone, best wishes, Bowie99". Waah!!!

The next morning we went back to the hotel to wait for him to leave and after a friend gave him a present, she also took the first photo of David and me.

WHAT SHALL I WEAR?

Billy Nevins, UK

I WAS JUST A WEE lad who had discovered Bowie and I'd been listening to anything of his I could get my hands on: *Space Oddity, The Man Who Sold The World, Aladdin Sane* and even *Images*. I was in love with his voice and music; he was new, he was fresh and most of all he was different. To my adolescent mind he was inspirational. Of course, at the time, it was still in the early days of the dynamic career that lay ahead. Tangent is a word that I hold dear — for me that word is a concise description of David's career.

In a ticket office in London's West End, I saw the posters on the wall: David Bowie Live at The Empire Pool London. I was so excited! I had my money in my hand and the guy behind the counter had the tickets. I had never seen Bowie and this was my dream. I gave him the money and got a ticket — he had handed me the gold dust, my first David Bowie concert ticket!

Then, like a teenage girl preparing for the prom, I thought — my god! What shall I wear? Ziggy? Duke? Aladdin? Which way to go?

I already had it in my head that, as I adored the *Midnight Special 1980 Floor Show*, I would dress that way. I started to accumulate relevant items of clothing.

I was a young boy back then and trying to buy a boob tube

was not easy, so my girlfriend Rosalinda helped out and bought me one. We then bought some beautiful gold gloves and attached some false nails (painted crimson) to either side, left and right of the torso. Left boob, right boob.

"Not quite enough," she said to me.

"Why?" I asked.

"You need skinny trousers like David," came the reply.

So I ended up with a pair of turquoise pajama bottoms; things are looking great, skin tight and I have legs like matches. Then my friend Mandy, who was Bowie mad, said "You need a cape." I was horrified at the thought of looking like Superman.

"No, you need a cape like Ziggy." She said

"Ok Mandy, I'll wear a cape." Out comes an old net curtain and I'm starting to blush.

Then the pair of them looked at my feet. "God forbid, you can't wear those old pumps, you need *boots*!" So they found a pair of 'break your ankle boots' like the ones Slade would wear.

I think the job is done. Rosalinda thinks not.

"Billy, you must wear this fox fur, you'll look beautiful."

All that was left was the makeup.

It was a night I will never forget....the Wembley Wizard did indeed touch the dial that night. Magnificent.

I ended up in *Melody Maker* described as the "Space Cowboy" or something similar!

MY BONKERS
WELSH FRIEND
Wendy Norman, UK

⟋⟍T A HOUSE PARTY one Saturday in October 1999, I struck up a conversation with someone about Bowie. He was generously offered a ticket for the Net Aid concert at Wembley. I was happy about this, because the day before I had been given a ticket for the television show *TFI Friday* at Riverside studios. I had been told by a friend that David Bowie was scheduled to appear on the show. You can imagine my excitement, as the nearest I had ever been was to say "Hi Dave" at a Tin Machine gig at the National Ballroom Kilburn in 1989. I was literally right at the front of the stage that hot, sweaty night; but sadly, David didn't even notice me.

A friend and I attended the filming of *TFI Friday*, but Bowie wasn't anywhere to be seen. I assumed he was going to appear from his dressing room and didn't want to mingle with the crowd. I was so disappointed and thought perhaps he'd cancelled, because he didn't appear. We had a good time anyway and particularly enjoyed Buster Rhymes.

A week later the same friend from Live TV telephoned to say, "Bowie is definitely on *TFI Friday* tonight, can you go? I put you on the guest list." I said, "Totally! I'm there like an hour ago!"

So I, and my bonkers Welsh friend Jeanette, rush to Riverside studios again. We were on the guest list, so we made our way to the hospitality area. I can't recall who we saw mooching about, because I was so nervous about being close to Bowie. So we sailed around trying to look like we belong when my friend Jeanette says, "Oh look, I do know who he is. I love his music!" I turned to see Bowie slowly making his way through the crowd and he's walking right towards us!

David looked gorgeous in jeans and a pastel jumper, his hair was long and beautiful and he looked so young. My heart was thumping in my chest as he neared us. I thought I'm just going to say "Hi Dave" and leave it at that. He was walking right past us when my friend grabbed his arm and said to him, "I love your music, I do." Bowie didn't react to being grabbed, he just smiled and said "thank you."

My friend then says, "I've got loads of your records, my favorite is (and she starts singing) "...*this is not my beautiful house, this is not my wife, how did I get here?*" Bowie simply said, "Wrong David," and walked away! I could have died right there. My friend said, "What's wrong with him?"

The show was great and Bowie was on form. I set my video recorder and watched it later and I ended up having a great weekend watching Net Aid too!

It was just a shame that my friend thought he was David Byrne of Talking Heads. To this day she still says, "What did he mean, 'wrong David'?"

BOWIE, ALDO BAGLI AND I

Patrizia Pezzola, Italy

$\mathcal{O}$N THE LATE 1970S I was a naïve teenager, desperately in love with David Bowie and his amazing music. My friend and I used to buy the weekly music magazine *Ciao 2001* to find out what our favorite icon was doing next. Soon we discovered that all the articles on Bowie were written by a young journalist name Aldo Bagli. Aldo was definitely a huge Bowie fan. His articles were full of admiration and respect for the Thin White Duke. We decided to write Aldo a letter.

Quite unexpectedly, I received a letter back from Aldo. It was a nice, polite letter and Aldo said he was happy to know that there were people who loved the same artists that he did. I was in heaven! On top of that he added that David was a good friend of his as they shared common scientific interests. They used to recommend books to each other on that topic. As time went on, I still followed David's career and his rare public appearances. I often wondered if Aldo was still in the music business and if he had continued his friendship with David.

Sadly enough, I discovered that Aldo Bagli died very young. I will always be very thankful to him for promoting David's work so carefully and relentlessly in the 1970s. I like to think that now, with David's passing, they've had a reunion and enjoyed spending time talking and discussing all the things they loved…over there in the sky.

Ciao David, ciao Aldo. Thank you.

DAVID HAS JUST
LEFT HIS HOTEL
Mike Gately, UK

$\mathcal{B}$ACK IN EARLY 1997 while listening to National Radio One in the UK, the two hosts of the flagship breakfast show (who did their show in Manchester and not London) said that the following morning they had David Bowie coming into the studio with a big announcement!

Putting two and two together, I went down to the BBC on Oxford Road, Manchester the next day. There was a crowd of about 20 people waiting. I'm sure I heard someone say, "David has just left his hotel." The excitement grew more and more. Sure enough, a Mercedes car pulled up and out of the car came my hero, Mr. David Bowie! I managed to move halfway up the stairs to get his autograph then, as I realized he was stopping for photos, I made my way around and back to the top of the stairs to have a photo taken with me when he got to the top.

He was so full of fun, and he even made a joke about the guy I asked to take the photo. David then went into the radio station and announced that he would be playing some very small, intimate gigs through the UK that summer! Mainly student unions!

I was so lucky to get tickets for the gig that July as there were less than 1,200 people there that hot summer night! Out of the eight tours that I saw of David's, this was the most special one. The Earthling Tour was awesome and getting to meet him and being able to see him perform at such a small venue was amazing. The next day, as my wife picked my clothes up from the chair in our bedroom, she asked "Was it raining last night? Your clothes are wet through!". "No," I replied. "It was just baking hot in there!"

David had asked us after the second song – "Are you hot yet?'

The crowd said "Yeah!"

David then asked "Are you really hot yet?"

Again, the crowd said "Yeah!"

To which David replied, "Well in two hours' time you're gonna be f★★★ing hot!"

And he was true to his word!

It was a wonderful show on a glorious night. Thank you David. XX

CLOSE ENCOUNTER
WITH A SUPERMAN
RaMoana, USA

ALTHOUGH MY ENCOUNTER WITH David Bowie was brief (about 5 minutes), in many ways it was prophetic and profound for me. I should explain that before the 1997 concerts I attended (Philadelphia October 3 and October 4 and Fort Lauderdale October 8), I awoke from a most vivid dream and the only one I had ever had about Bowie at the time. Three days before the October 3 concert, I sat straight up in bed at 6:30 am, smiling and actually woke up AMan (aka Action Man aka my husband) and told him I had the coolest dream *ever*!

The Dream

A group of people all went towards a large door that was locked and tried to enter the building. I went alone, more to the left, around the building and found a smaller door which was unlocked. I could hear David Bowie's voice and I opened the door which went to a small hallway that led to a larger room that looked like a warehouse with open beams on the ceiling. To the right of the hallway was a small room where Bowie was talking on the phone. I walked straight past him so as not to interrupt and into the warehouse. I stood in front of a small wooden counter in the center of the room and, by this time, the rest of the group had entered through the larger door and were talking to Gail Ann Dorsey and others from the band. Bowie came down the hallway and went to the other side of the counter, joked around with some of us and finally said, "Right, I guess we should give them our autographs" and gave us all autographs on paper they had produced. That was basically the dream which freaked me out when Bowie friend Frippertronic (Micke) told me he too had a vivid Bowie dream! Fripp's dream was almost identical to mine: from the windows, to the warehouse-like room, to the wooden counter Bowie stood behind! In Fripp's dream, he had gone through the larger door with the group. He even woke straight up from bed like I had and told one of his mates about the dream because it was so vivid and detailed. Imagine the chill bumps I got when Fripp told me the time he had the dream in Sweden (which is six hours ahead) was at 12:30 — exactly the time I had my dream! I got more chill bumps when I arrived at the Electric Factory on October 3 and saw the windows on the side of the building were identical to the ones in my dream. I told Fripp a bit more about the dream which I had interpreted as "I would need to find Bowie for myself."

The Concert

The October 3, 1997 concert in Philadelphia was awesome and was my first Bowie concert. I could not imagine the recordings of his songs would be that much more powerful live! The October 4 concert was different for me in that A Man joined us and I stood further back, behind the control station. I got the full effect of the light show and the videos (I saw the full, real versions of the porn show and the other projections behind Bowie on stage on the small control screens. The set list was also in full view). All

in all, the Philadelphia experience was great, made even greater
by meeting all the Teenage Wildlifers and partying afterwards on
October 4. I did not get to meet Bowie at this point.

I flew back to Florida that Sunday morning after staying up all
night (only three hours sleep in three days). I cried and laughed
all the way home from the airport (AMan was off travelling for a
couple of days so I was on my own), missing all the great people
I met and wanting them with me! I knew AMan and I would
go to the Ft. Lauderdale show thinking it probably wouldn't
be as fun. We almost decided not to go! Wednesday, October
8 finally arrived; we drove to Ft Lauderdale in three hours and
went straight to the venue (The Chili Pepper) at 1:00 p.m., just
to see what it was like and if people were already in line. We saw
RobotMonster there and were pleased to see the venue was small.
We checked in at the motel and went back to get in line at The
Chili Pepper. There were others that were ahead of us in line (only
about ten people total) and I met Kelley C., Hans M., and some
others who told me about the October 7 show the night before and
that Bowie had come into the side of the building, just around the
corner from where we were in line. Bowie also had come outside
after the sound check to sign autographs. I had AMan hold the
line for me and hung out at the end of the building, just hoping to
get a glimpse and a quick photo of Bowie going from his vehicle
and into the building. At about 3:30 or 4-ish, a few equipment
busses started arriving, parking on the side of the street and we
waited for any signs of Bowie-life. Kelley had been allowed to
shoot photos inside the Chili Pepper the night before and had
great shots of Bowie. She brought her *Aladdin Sane* album cover
to get signed — inside the cover where the full shot of Bowie was
— and we joked that if he signed that, she should hang it over her
bed. A few hours went by and still no Bowie — we also realized
he might not need to do a sound check since he played the night
before. Security put up a few barriers and I chatted up one of the

security guards who was standing there. He told me that they had blown out the speakers the night before and the crew had been there early in the morning setting up 12 new speakers. Chances were that a sound check would be in order! He also told me that the next show in Atlanta would be a "pit stop".

After an endless wait, the tour bus pulled up, more barriers went up and one security guy told us to move back to the end of the building and that Bowie definitely was *not* on the bus, "I promise you." I tell Tia: "this means Bowie IS on that bus!" After a long while, Gail Ann Dorsey got off the bus and walked straight to the courtyard of the Chili Pepper, not even turning her head in our direction.

I did not notice Mike Garson getting off the bus, but I believe he was next off. Then all of sudden a blonde girl, Reeves Gabrels, and Bowie got off the bus! Gabrels kept walking but Bowie came over to us smiling and looking so fine! I purposely decided I would stand back, not rush Bowie, and just take a few snaps high above everyone's head as I was in the back of the maddening crowd. I had never been a fan or follower of anyone to know how these things worked or even what to bring to sign. I had grabbed my *Outside* tape cover from the car earlier. It seemed like time stood still when suddenly I was pushed up to where Bowie was, right in front of him (only the railed waist-high barrier between us) and no one was behind me! It was like I was in a protective bubble with Bowie — no one was touching or shoving me for five minutes! It was all rather surreal; Bowie grabbed my hand to calm my shock, I suspect. I still do not know how he signed my *Outside* tape cover and held my hand at the same time!

Later I realized there was a voice in my head while I was being pushed in front of Bowie and it was my brother Bill's voice (he had passed away six months before to the day, on April 8th 1997) and I heard him say "No way you are going to miss this!" So I have my brother Bill to thank for this extraordinary event that changed my life! It was Bowie and his music that got me through losing my brother before all this. I don't believe I would have survived the year without finding the *TeenageWildlife* fan site and becoming a fan of Bowie and getting into his music. *Outside* had already "spoken to me," showed me the dark side, but somehow Bowie got you through it, and made it okay.

Back to the moment — I tried to be cool and was not going to say anything, but I ended up blurting out really loud — "You are the greatest visionary of our time!" Bowie laughed, of course! I was awestruck at this point and did not know what to say, so I took a bunch of pictures, practically up his nose! Someone was asking if he would do his newer stuff and if he would do "Changes" and he answered him though I can't recall exactly what he said. I told Bowie he was brilliant and that we loved him (bigger smile) and then he was rushed into the building.

I galloped back to A Man, jumping and laughing and shaking. I went back to the car and tried to compose myself and shook for about ten minutes. I put up my camera, not wanting to risk losing the film if I took it inside the venue (having already experienced the loss of a throwaway camera in Philly!). The wait in line began and the sound check started. "I'm Deranged" was played and a hilarious Country/Western version of "Scary Monsters" (Johnny Cash version). We finally got inside and I went forward, standing right in front of Bowie to witness the LEGENDARY 3 hour and 45 minutes, 36-song concert! I knew we were in for the ultimate when he came out and asked, "Do you want a short or a long set? You gotta minute?" I pushed my hands further and further apart and shouted "Looonnnnggg" (of course!) And he warned us to call our mamas — we would be there until Saturday!

The concert was awesome, highlighted for me by:

When Pigs Could Fly

I had a few things to throw during some of the songs (it was a *TeenageWildlife* thing —think Rocky Horror — paper airplanes flown during "O Superman," seven dwarfs were tossed during "Little Wonder"). I was the only one there to do such a thing at this show, and at the surprise meeting before the show I had showed Bowie my bag of stuff (moondust for "Hallo Spaceboy," 'oh Ramoana' panties for "Hearts Filthy Lesson," beanie pig for "Seven Years In Tibet") and said "if you like, I can give this to you now!" Bowie looked inside the bag and laughed! During "Seven Years In Tibet" I was waiting for the "when pigs can fly" line, so my beanie pig could fly but then I realized I could accidentally throw it right into his sax and muffle it! I was that close and this was a small venue, so I tossed it underhand so it slid across the stage and landed by his foot. He picked it up after the song ended, looked at Gail Ann Dorsey and said "it's mine" and hugged it! Then I noticed Gail had a whole pig family collection already on her amp. I did ask her in a chat years later if she still had her pig collection, and she said yes! I also saw my pig in a photo at another '97 show: my beanie pig went on tour!

Bowie sang spread-legged over my RaMOANa sequined panties ("Oh RaMOANa" was sequined on the front, and "HFL" was sequined on the back of these purple George t-back panties from England I had) which I had thrown during Hearts Filthy Lesson (during "oh Ramona, if there was only something between us, other than our clothes"). Other highlights: touching Reeves guitar, AMan getting a piece of the floating eyeball and all of us covered in moondust. The band also made impressions etched on my memory: Gail Ann Dorsey singing "O Superman" to a girl on her Dad's shoulders, Mike Garson zoned out with his mouth open performing "V2-Schneider," and Reeves Gabrel's shredding on his guitar.

I loved watching the superman have the greatest time performing and giving so much to his fans — Bowie talked to us a lot between the two breaks and the whole concert was like he was challenging us, trying to blow us off our numbing feet and at the end of it all, he appreciated we hung in there with him every step of the way. We were exhausted and dehydrated but totally blown away by this awesome concert-marathon! It was so hot that at one point we did get sprayed with water and a girl near us passed out and had to be carried off. Several of us yelled our thanks to Bowie and he also thanked us.

We could not help but wonder about Bowie — the artistry in his lyrics and music notwithstanding, what was he getting out of all this? The man could not be making any money from these concerts (1,000, possibly 1,500, people at $45 a head at this venue! It might be enough to pay security!). The way he was enjoying every minute of it and smiling and talking to us, the concert was both intimate and awe-inspiring and is the longest Bowie show in history! The whole experience was cathartic, surreal and so much more than I could imagine.

We got home and AMan showed me the *Earthling* CD cover. Bowie stands in a tattered Union Jack jacket, but he *looks forward*. Look at the back of the cover and "you" stand in the same position as Bowie with the same view, but photo-reversed. Are you are standing in his "shoes"? Is he standing with us? We should look forward? (Then AMan tells me *Earthling*, unscrambled spells 'Real Thing' ha!). Bowie leads us to *think* but does not tell us what to think. I had found Bowie. We continue to discover more "Bowieness" in his music, lyrics, live shows, Bowie fans and we crave for more!

Since these shows, I've always said, "I'm addicted to seeing David Bowie live, I could live in a Bowie concert, just throw me whisky and water and I will be fine!" AMan first saw Bowie live at Madison Square Garden in 1978. After AMan and I met, I moved to England and we married and he played me all his Bowie vinyl.

We ended up seeing about 30 shows, eight in Europe. Amsterdam 2004 was our last Bowie show, and quite an experience too, with our Amsterdamned After Party. I may have also seen the second longest Bowie show in history in Dublin 2003 with 33 songs! I know people that have seen over a hundred David Bowie shows, but it doesn't matter if you saw him live once or many times, it was never enough! You still wanted to go to another Bowie show, it was the greatest high! It was the most brilliant, exciting times of our lives and we will always treasure the many experiences. Paying forward all he has given me is what I have attempted to do; he really is an indelible part of each of us and forever an inspiration. I have always been fascinated by how Bowie has inspired others. I think there is still so much to explore and discover from this artist who knew no boundaries and gave so much to his craft. Bowie is the epitome of "art" in all his works. He did his homework, and so should we!

Many thanks to:

AMan for the proper introduction to Bowie's music and all the clever, cryptic bits and deep thoughts AMan notices concerning Bowie and for holding the queue for me and my handbag (Roseland, NYC could be 12 or 14 hour queue times and we saw all of the shows in 2000 and 2002);

Teenagewildlife, which was our first playground and where we got our nicknames. This was the innovative, interactive and first social media site on the net;

BowieNet, and all the interesting and sometimes kooky fans;

Phil Kushnir of LG73/Max Radio that has let me play all the Bowie I want for ten years now and my listeners of my weekly Bowie radio program, who keep me on my toes and give me more Bowie education that I could imagine; and

The amazing, inspirational, wonderful (and so much more) David Bowie.

1. "My Most Treasured Possession" (White)

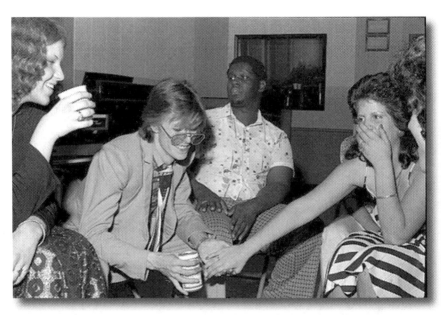

2. Patti Brett, David Bowie, Luther Vandross, Marla Kanevsky, Sigma Sound Studios, Philadelphia, PA 1974. (Photo by Dagmar)

3. "Sigma Kids" Philadelphia Mural Art (S. Powers)

4. "Young Americans" Philadelphia Mural Art (S. Powers)

5. "Patty Bowie" Philadelphia Mural Art (S. Powers)

6. "David Live" Philadelphia Mural Art (S. Powers)

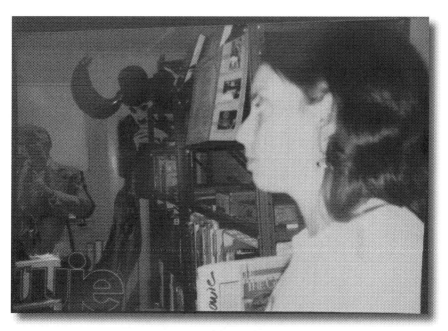

7. The Bowie Room (J. Stoller)

8. Potsdam 2003 (B. Streun)

9. Premier Ticket 1979 (S. Lock)

10. David and Simone, Dublin, 1999 (S. Metge)

11. David & Mike, 1997 (M. Gately)

12. Manchester Ticket, 1997 (M. Gately)

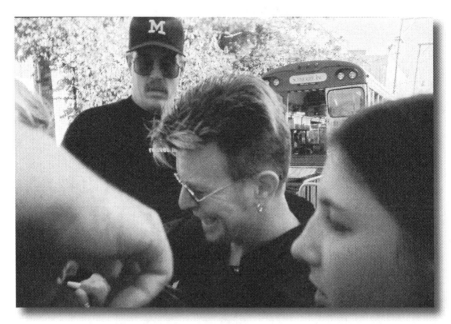

13. The Chili Pepper, Ft. Lauderdale, FL 1997 (RaMoana)

14. The Chili Pepper, Ft. Lauderdale, FL 1997 (RaMoana)

15. The Chili Pepper, Ft. Lauderdale, FL 1997 (RaMoana)

16. The Chili Pepper, Ft. Lauderdale, FL 1997 (RaMoana)

MOMENTS IN TIME

We met in January 1978; the first conversation we ever had was about our love for Bowie.

Sandra (Spidey) Atkins, UK

I have been a fan since 1972, when I was 11 years of age. In 1990 I was front and center at a show in Ottawa, Canada. David Bowie was right in front of me. I held his hand through a few songs, and as he was right there and for no other reason than that, I held his ankle for a while. My kids still make fun of me saying that I gave David Bowie a "wankle!"

Ray Nash, Canada

We were at the Roseland Ballroom show in September 1996 and David looked out into the audience at one point and saw us. "I know you, and you… and you," he said as he pointed to us. "I know ALL of you!" It was my 100th Bowie show and I was thrilled beyond belief that he acknowledged those of us from Philly. A little later in the show, David announced he was doing a song from the new album. "Earthlings, Earthling. I'm not sure." He looked down at us and asked, "What do you think?" We all yelled, "Earthling." "Earthling it is," he said. And at the end of the show, several people handed me a cake with candles ablaze that had "100" on it. I'll never forget that night.

Patti Brett, USA

My sisters and I had tickets for David Bowie at Milton Keynes Bowl for the Sound and Vision tour in 1990. My favorite song that I just could not miss was "Heroes." Having had a little beer, my sister Sheila and I had to use the loo but, with "Heroes" in mind, we just couldn't leave to queue up. Instead we saw some trees and decided to be discreet. Sure enough, mid-way through our mission, we heard *"I, I will be king and you, you will be my queen..."* We ran back as fast as we could, laughing all the way. The best day of our lives!

Alyson Lewis, UK

Every band I played in I tried to apply a "No Bowie Covers" rule....because we always sucked and it would be almost sacrilegious to f★★★ up his music like that!

Randy Marthins, USA

I don't have a Tin Machine memory as such — other than being in the front row, right underneath David during "Heaven's In Here." That is a *good* memory!!!

Jean Marie Dawson, Scotland

We had tickets for the Serious Moonlight tour at the Spectrum in Philadelphia. The seats were on the floor, near the back. The usher came to us and said that we couldn't sit there because it was right behind the soundboard. They moved us up to the 11th row, center! *That* show was fan-friggin-tastic! *Church On Time* indeed!!!!

Johnny Quest, USA

One of my favorite David Bowie photos I ever took was on my birthday, 18 October 2003, in Frankfurt, Germany. This was during "Bring Me the Disco King," although with my ultra-zoom camera I felt I was intruding on a private moment! The Frankfurt show was my best birthday ever, involving celebrations with many fans that night both before and after the show. The bonus was Bowie humping my birthday balloon and then kicking it off the stage!

RaMoana, USA

I was walking in a double file line home from school in Northeast Philadelphia. The nuns walked us to the traffic light this way. I was in the 6th grade, the spring of 1972. My friend Beth who was walking in front of me started singing the new hit "*Ch... ch....ch...changes, turn and face the strange...*" When I got home and changed my uniform I headed to the record store and bought the 45 r.p.m. record. It was love at first sight! I wasn't allowed to go to the Tower Theater, so my first show was at the Spectrum in 1974!

Dorothy Kulisek, USA

Travelling across Germany to Berlin in order to attend a David Bowie tribute party, my friends and I stayed at a small hostel. Without expecting any particular miracles to happen just yet, we each chose a bunk bed. As soon as I sat down on the bed that I choose, I froze in disbelief. Written on the bed post was the message "David Bowie is the Captain of my Life." I wished the artist behind the stylized sharpie scripture had left their name, but unfortunately we never got to hear the other half of this bed post's story.

Melanie Krichel, Germany

"You little wonder, you…" his brow furrowed as his gaze swung around to me. "Who threw that gnome?!" Bowie was looking straight at me….because my friend behind me had hit him in the bollocks with one of the seven dwarves! Bowie laughed and gave us a boyish smile, scooping up one of the other dwarves that we had flung onto the stage. He chatted with the audience with the dwarf perched on the mic stand!

Gwenn Catterfeld, USA

Tickets for the Glass Spider Tour in Philadelphia went on sale Saturday morning. As was my custom in those days (before "Casual Fridays") I went to work, then Happy Hour at Doc Watson's (I lost Doobies Bar in the "divorce"), closing at Doc Watson's, then the post closing hang-out at The Savoy. At an appropriate time, I left the Savoy and took the subway down to the box office at JFK (or was it the Vet?). I was waiting on line and watching the sun come up over the stadium. It was a pretty cool experience as I had never "camped out" for tickets before. Doing it in suit and tie *with* my briefcase? I'm sure David would have appreciated it!

Randy Marthins, USA

A fan since *Aladdin Sane* in 1972, I bunked off school and went to Victoria Station. They told us if we behaved ourselves, David would come and talk to us when he arrived. Unfortunately, David didn't talk to us, but we did see him and received a free *Station to Station* LP! Forty years later, I'm trying to get some of my grandkids into the best music ever!

Debbie Pagel, UK

In April 1978 my three friends and I had tickets for the
Heroes Tour at the Spectrum in Philadelphia. Our seats were
in the upper level (nose bleed section) yet we were in the first
row. I was in the tenth grade and while we had been to many
concerts these were the worst seats we had ever gotten. But we
were thrilled to be going to see the Bowie show. The night
of the show, my buddies were upset because they were unable
to score some weed. There had been a major drug bust earlier
in the week and all the regular suppliers were out of product.
We got to our seats and we were way, way up there! The stage
looked so far away. When the lights went out and the show was
about to start, the Spectrum crowd started their ritual of "firing
up!" As the show progressed, there was so much smoke where
we were sitting that it was like a layer of fog — a marijuana fog
— which made it even harder to see the stage and the fog kept
rising right toward our seating area. As we spent most of the
show completely immersed in the fog, my friends who so much
wanted to get high, were on cloud nine. To this day, each of us
still remembers how we got the best "free" high courtesy of our
fellow Bowie fans.

Dave Wisniewski, USA

My first real recollection of David Bowie is from 1985.
He made a cameo on the *Looney Tunes 50th Anniversary Special.*
He was being chased down a corridor towards an elevator by
a camera, apparently being pestered by questions about Bugs
Bunny. He insisted that "I can't and I won't talk about Bugs
Bunny." He initially denied knowing him, but finally said that
he knew him…and might be doing an album with him. Finally,
once safe in the elevator, he confessed that Bugs saved his life
once. "I was swimming one day, I got the cramps, he dives in
the water, saves me and saves my girlfriend. Then he runs off

with my girlfriend! I don't take women around him anymore."
Bugs Bunny. What a cad!

Mark W. Falzini, USA

Remembering David Bowie at the Tower Theater in Upper
Darby, PA — The Ziggy tour was a complete game changer for
everyone in attendance. It was mind bending, ear splitting and hair
raising. But most of all…it was f★★★ing brilliant! And I have to
be sure to give a mention to the opening band of the evening —
Fumble! It was Jerry Lee Lewis on steroids and the crowd loved
them! Bless you, David Bowie. You are, and will always be, truly
missed.

Bob Wigo, USA

After sitting outside on the ground for hours at the Electric
Factory in Philadelphia, it was a pleasure to learn that the office
in the factory next door had a bathroom that no one minded if we
used. A few of us ventured out of line to make use of the facilities.
All went well right up until we tried to leave the building — we
were locked in! Trying several doors, we ended up in the factory
part of the building — catwalks and all — and by this time we
could hear the sound check coming from the venue next door!
At one point we were in an open area with a concrete wall, high
above ground level and I could look out and see the parking lot
where my friends were still in line. We waved and screamed,
but no one could hear us and certainly no one was looking up at
the next building. It was only ten or fifteen minutes, but I had
visions of "hearing" David Bowie sing but never actually seeing
him perform that night! Finally, we came upon a back door that

opened and we were able to exit into the alley. Did my friend miss me? Nope — didn't even notice I was gone.

dkp, USA

A few days ago one of our friends went back to the Brixton mural. She told me that a little boy had gone past with his mother; he looked at the mural and the flowers laid in front of it (yes, still fresh flowers and tributes being left there daily) and asked his Mum, "what happened?" My friend was really upset when she heard his Mum reply, "He got old." He *didn't* get old, he wasn't old at all! When I relayed this story to my husband, Don, he reacted very differently. Don said, "How wonderful that the little boy asked that, rather than 'why is that man wearing makeup?' David Bowie changed the world and that's the only world that little lad knows." We have so much to be thankful for.

Sandra (Spidey) Atkins, UK

17. Sandra (Spidey) and Don, The Hammersmith Apollo, 2002 (S. Atkins)

18. "Bring Me the Disco King", Frankfurt,
Germany, October 2003 (RaMoana)

19. The Bedpost, Berlin, Germany 2016 (M. Krechel)

20. David & the Gnome, Washington, D.C., 1997 (G. Cattenfeld)

21. Washington, D.C., 1997 (G. Cattenfeld)

22. David's Young Fans (D. Pagel)

23. Jasmine and Bowie (J. Storm)

24. Karon Bihari (F. Moriarty)

25. David and Zane, 1997 (M. Kanevsky)

26. "Sailor" (S. Metge)

27. "Bowie Netters" (S. Metge)

28. Patti & Carlos, 1995, Doobies Bar,
Philadelphia, PA (P. Brett)

29. David & Zane, 1995 Reunion (M. Kanevsky)

30. Bowie Tattoo (M. Moyer)

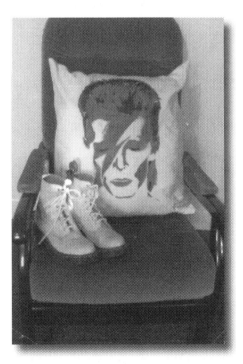

31. Bowie Chair "Moon Blue" (T. Bradley)

32. David and Sandra (Spidey), 2002 (S. Atkins)

**33. Patti and Carlos, 2016, NYC, The Cutting
Room Bowie Tribute (P. Brett)**

34. Blackstar/Sigma Kid Tattoo (N. Webster)

**35. David Bowie, Lazarus Premier, NYC,
December 7, 2015 (B. Strun)**

THROUGH THE
DECADES

THE YEAR OF THE DIAMOND DOGS AND MORE

Patti Brett, USA

1974 SAW THE RETURN of David Bowie to the Tower Theater to promote his new album *Diamond Dogs*. I was excited that he would be performing again, just three blocks from my house! I hoped I would have an opportunity to meet him again.

I had just started working for Midnight Sun Concerts at the Tower about a month prior to the Bowie concert announcement, but I "camped out" for tickets anyway. The tickets were to go on sale May 10th. I had finals the day before, so as soon as I finished at school I headed to the Tower to get in line. My two friends, Debbie and Danny, were first in line. Leslie and Marla were already there as well, along with several others I didn't know. I took my place and met Taylor and Jim who were in line in front of me. I was the eleventh person in the queue and hoped that I could still get a front row orchestra pit seat, but I was pretty far back in the line.

During the course of the evening, more people arrived — Charlie, Dale and Brad — and everyone discussed their anticipation of the new album. It seemed like an eternity to wait, but finally

155

the box office opened and we were able to purchase our tickets. I don't remember exactly what seats I bought, but my friend and I pooled our tickets together and came up with tickets for four nights — Monday, Wednesday, Thursday and Friday. Tickets for the Tuesday night show were transferred from a cancelled T. Rex show, so I already had tickets for that night.

Shortly after we purchased the tickets, Peter (my supervisor from the Tower) called to ask what Bowie shows I would be working. I explained that I had tickets for the shows and I wasn't planning on working any of them. I was told that if I didn't work the shows, I would no longer be employed by Midnight Sun Concerts. This was my *dream* job, and I was quite upset. Peter said he would get back to me a week before the shows to find out what I had decided.

I drove myself crazy trying to figure out how to get out of working, while still keeping my job. A friend of the family was a nurse and she suggested I put a cast on my leg, which would remedy my dilemma. She brought home all the items I needed for the cast. In the 70s, plaster was still used for casts — and it was now July — but I was determined to keep my job and still see David at all the shows. Our nurse friend came to the house one evening and the cast was put on my left leg so that I could still drive. The plan was to keep the cast on for the week.

When Peter called to ask if I would be working the shows, I told him I had been in an accident and was in a cast up to my knee. He laughed and said that was very convenient, but understood it wasn't possible for me to work with a cast. I had accomplished my goal!

The week finally arrived and we attended the shows — me in my cast. We had made our clothes for the show and gathered at my house to all walk to the theater together. It was really warm and the cast was really hot. By Thursday, I couldn't take the itching and sweating, so I put my leg in the shower and let the water make the plaster soft. I cut the cast off with a steak knife!

My story was safe for years, until I related it to a journalist that was writing a story for a local newspaper magazine shortly before the "Let's Dance" tour in 1983. One of the first people I ran into at the show was an old boss, Rick Green, who greeted me with "oh…I broke my leg!"

THERE'S A STAR MAN

Linda A. Metz, USA

I WAS OBSESSED WITH MUSIC since the Beatles first appeared on Ed Sullivan when I was seven, and as I moved into my teen years I was an avid reader of all the fan and rock magazines. When I first started seeing pictures of Bowie in the early 1970s, I was mesmerized. He really seemed to be from another world, unlike the long haired hippiesque bands that crawled out of the 1960s and into the next decade. I wore out the *Ziggy Stardust* album and swore I had to see him in person!

In 1972, I was in 10th grade when I heard that David Bowie and the Spiders from Mars were actually coming to Philadelphia, just over the bridge from my suburban home in New Jersey! My best friend and I went to the Wanamaker's department store to buy tickets and there were about 50 people in line. The night of the concert, we cajoled my father to drive us to Philly. It was way up to 69th Street and Market we went, to the now famous Tower Theater, dressed in our own version of "glam" (velvet bell bottoms, black bodysuit with green stars for me!). I sat through the evening completely entranced by David, Mick Ronson and the Spiders as they put on a show unlike any other. We talked of nothing else for weeks.

In 1973, I bought the *Aladdin Sane* album and ran to my

friend's house to lie on the floor, reading the lyrics and sighing over his famous "lightning bolt" portrait on the cover. Soon after, in 1973, he took over the *Midnight Special* to put on the *1980 Floor Show* treating everyone who watched TV to his latest incarnation. Five of my friends and I gathered together to watch and exclaim over yet another side of Bowie.

From that time on I went to every local concert through all his changes including "The Thin White Duke" period, his *Young Americans* days of which the album was recorded in Philly, and his *Man Who Fell to Earth* crazy cocaine days when he also appeared on the Dick Cavett Show. I never missed any chance to see Bowie.

When I was in my twenties, I found my dream job working at a record distribution company. This was followed by many years of working in the music industry with various artists and labels. Through all that, Bowie was the one person I always wanted to meet. I had several "almost happened" moments, including when he released the *Tin Machine* album and my sister and I attended a press event where he was to be the guest of honor. Bowie came in and was besieged by people. He turned and left before getting half way through the room.

I moved to Los Angeles for a few years and when I moved back east to New York in the late 1990s, I heard that Bowie was living in the Village and going to shows here and there. The night I moved into my new apartment, I was supposed to go to a show at Irving Plaza and was still unpacking so I decided to miss the opening act, Placebo. When I finally got to the club my co-workers said, "Oh, you just missed Bowie. He was on stage with Placebo. He just left." Needless to say, I was bereft.

In early 2002, I was working at Columbia Records when a friend called my office to say "guess who just got out of the elevator!" Yes, it was David Bowie. The label decided to have a luncheon with him to introduce his long awaited *Heathen* release, which was influenced by the 9/11 attacks and was Bowie's 22nd album. All of the buyers and executives of the (then) major retailers like Tower, Virgin, HMV were invited to meet Bowie and hear the new record. Everyone was able to take pictures and chat. At age 55 he looked fantastic in a gold silk suit. When it came time for me to meet him, finally after all these years, I reverted to a 15 year old girl and just started yammering about how much I loved him, his music and anything to do with him. He took me by the shoulders, looked me in the eyes and just said "I understand."

AND THERE WON'T BE ANY TROUBLE

Frank Moriarty, USA

ON 1977, I HAD several years of rock and roll photography under my belt and was also beginning to establish myself as a writer, contributing pieces to various publications including the Philadelphia "alternative" weekly *The Drummer*. My editor there was David Fricke, now one of the most respected music writers and a senior editor at *Rolling Stone*.

As I was living in the Philadelphia area, I'd begun shooting a number of the best original area bands. Kenn Kweder and His Secret Kidds, Alan Mann and the Free Arts Band, and Johnny's Dance Band were among the musicians I shot at venues ranging from the grimy Hot Club to the higher-profile Bijou Café. Through connections in the legendary bohemian area along Philadelphia's South Street, I got to know singer Karon Bihari, and soon became her photographer.

In this era, Karon was a force of nature. Over the months I shot her, her star was rising with cabaret shows at Reno Sweeney's in New York, and sold-out, multi-day stints at the Bijou.

Usually Karon's set was entirely cover songs rather than original material. Her stage show could range from ditzy character comedy to tragic drama, often in the space of one or two songs. The sets could include everything from the Young Rascal's "I Ain't Gonna Eat Out My Heart Any More" to The Kinks "Celluloid Heroes." But the one showpiece that truly stunned the crowds was always the same: The "Sweet Thing" suite from David Bowie's *Diamond Dogs* album. Karon had the ability to inhabit those dark lyrics and convey the song in moving fashion, and her strong band provided a perfect range of dynamics to help enhance that communication.

Working with Karon was always an adventure, and you never knew where you'd end up or who you'd meet. During the years I was hanging with Karon, I chatted with Divine, rode around Manhattan in a limousine with Bernie Taupin and shot *Saturday Night Live's* Laraine Newman singing backup vocals for Peter Allen at four in the morning behind the locked doors of Reno Sweeney's. Through the Karon connection, I did photos for Allen and Bette Midler's Harlettes, and Karon herself was the inspiration for Bruce Springsteen's "Candy's Room," the lyrics of which were an entirely accurate depiction of her Greenwich Village apartment in a building owned by Midler.

But above all, Karon loved David Bowie. "In Candy's room, there are pictures of her heroes on the wall," Springsteen sang. I can tell you that a large number of those photos were of Bowie.

Through her network of friends and acquaintances that spanned the clubs and venues of New York City, Karon had put out the word that meeting David was Priority One. And then one night the call came — David was at the club Hurrah on 62nd Street, and was willing to meet her. By now well aware that anything could happen when around Karon, I was happy that I had just reloaded on film earlier that day. I had my camera bag and away we sped uptown.

We arrived somewhat breathlessly at Hurrah, terrified that perhaps David had tired of the club and moved on. Then again,

Hurrah was one of the epicenters of New York music's bleeding edge, hosting everyone from Suicide and Johnny Thunders to 8-Eyed Spy and Klaus Nomi. It would soon become notorious as the site of a bloody fight between Sid Vicious and Todd Smith, brother of Patti Smith. We entered off 62nd Street and ascended to the club level.

Entering the main room, there was the usual club chaos in the air. Off to the left the dance floor wound around, passing through columns to end at the stage. But a few feet straight ahead was a partitioned-off area, with two couches facing each other and a couple of chairs. The area was remarkable for two reasons: it was almost empty, and one of the few people in that area was clearly David Bowie.

I can't remember exactly who had brokered the meeting — possibly Ruth Polsky, or one of the club's influential DJs — but within moments Karon and I were being ushered into the sanctum. By this time I'd met or interviewed a fair number of rock stars, but I couldn't believe I was about to meet David. I was a massive fan of his work, having seen him live for the first time when he sang "All the Young Dudes" at Philadelphia's Tower Theater with Mott the Hoople. That was the night before his own two-show run opened at the same venue on the Spiders from Mars' first tour, shows which I surreptitiously photographed. I'd then seen — and photographed after smuggling in my camera gear — three more Spiders dates with the expanded band which included Mike Garson and the horn section. Getting those shots had required disassembling the camera to get past security: camera body in the underwear, lenses in the socks.

Now here I was in New York, camera gear intact, stepping into David Bowie's presence.

Until a large hand landed with a solid thud on my right shoulder. I turned to face a most imposing, sizeable African American gentleman. The expression on his face was not particularly welcoming. Without a word he crooked his finger at me and I began to reluctantly move away from David Bowie as he rose to say hello to Karon.

My new friend and I arrived in a corner. He silently pointed at my camera bag, covered with various backstage passes. I handed it to him. He opened it, took an inventory of the contents, closed it and handed it back to me. For a long moment he continued… just… looking…at.. me. Then he leaned over and, in an impossibly deep voice offered me advice:

"Don't open that. And there won't be any trouble."

At this point, disregarding those instructions was absolutely the furthest thing from my mind. Intimidation can work wonders.

He walked me back to the entrance of the cordoned area, and gave me a curt nod to enter.

To Karon's credit, she interrupted her conversation with David to introduce me. I don't recall all of the conversation thereafter, which I largely let Karon handle while I sat there content mostly to simply listen while in his presence. I do remember David being very nice, sincere and inclusive.

But my strongest memory is of the flashes of light reflected in the famously expanded pupil of David's left eye. Like most New York clubs, Hurrah was characterized by hyperactive lights flashing in a dizzying array of angles. At Hurrah this was even more pronounced by the heavy presence of mirrors throughout the club. So sitting with David presented me with fascinating but somewhat disconcerting hypnotic, strobe-like effects. They continually sparkled off his eye at irregular intervals. I'd have loved to try to capture it via available light photography — but, of course, I'd been warned in no uncertain terms. The camera stayed in the bag.

Spending time with David Bowie that night is one of my favorite memories of that era, though I did eventually move on to focus on writing rather than photography. But without that initial interest, I'd never have had this great opportunity.

Of course, within months of our meeting, David would enter Hurrah in a professional capacity as he utilized the club for the shooting of the "Fashion" promotional video.

BOWIE AND A CHOC-ICE

Stuart Dalzell, UK

Newcastle City Hall 14 June 1978

ON MID–FEBRUARY 1978, I'D heard on the grapevine that details of Bowie's new tour would be announced the following week in the music press. To ensure I got the best tickets I knew I needed to act fast. I also knew the promoters preferred postal orders as, unlike cheques, they didn't need to wait for the funds to clear. So in anticipation of the official announcement, I'd purchased a number of postal orders in varying denominations from my local post office, along with a collection of first class stamps. I thought I'd be able to get my applications in ahead of the crowd.

As time was of the essence, I hatched a plan to try and get a head start on all the Bowie hopefuls. I decided to ring the *New Musical Express* news desk on the Monday evening ahead of publication and pray that some kind soul would take pity on me and give me the ticket information over the phone.

My plan worked!

In fact, I'm convinced that the guy that helped me was the now famous Danny Baker. In any event, I had all the details I needed and was able to catch the first post on Tuesday morning.

I'd decided to go to all three Stafford Bingley Hall gigs and all three London Earl's Court gigs.

My six little white envelopes were duly dispatched to MAM Promotions, New Bond Street, London along with the obligatory stamped addressed envelope — one for each gig. I was prepared for a long wait as I remembered how it took two months for MAM to process tickets for Bowie's '76 Empire Pool Wembley gigs. However, this time I was pleasantly surprised!

I had gone to work as usual on Friday when I got a call around 10 am from my Mum. Blimey, I thought, what on earth has happened? "Stuart, the post has come and you've got lots of envelopes. I think they might be your Bowie tickets." I couldn't believe it! I'd only sent them on Tuesday.

I couldn't wait to get home and see what seats I'd gotten and was elated to find I had Block AA for all the Earl's Court gigs — row C first night, row D second night and row A for the final night! Front Row! I was in heaven. I'd obviously beaten the rush — so much so that my Bingley Hall tickets were all sent in one envelope with a note from the box office which just said "naughty." At least they'd realized I was a true fan and not a tout (scalper) — phew! Anyway, I had my tickets and was going to six shows. Yet there was still to be a surprise turn of events.

As background, the summer of 1978 was a particularly good year for big name gigs. Bowie, Dylan and Sinatra were all performing in the UK. I'd heard that the "Daily Mirror Pop Club" was running a competition to win tickets for all three artists. To stand a chance you had to complete a limerick:

> *When Bowie, Sinatra and Bob*
> *Auditioned for the very same job,*
> *Their notes were so sweet, They sounded a treat,*

So I entered the phrase: "So as punk rockers all
three lost the job!" — *and it won!*

I'd opted for Bowie at Newcastle City Hall on June 14 as
my preferred date as it was the opening night of the UK tour. I
couldn't believe my luck, especially when the tickets arrived and
they were front stalls. Amazing. So now I had tickets for seven
shows.

We had worked out that we could get an overnight train back
to London on the same night. *The Daily Mirror* was paying for our
travel but not accommodations, so we opted to save money and
return to London that same night. I had guessed this venue would
be small, but once inside I realized how special this gig was going
to be. It's a mystery why Bowie had picked such a tiny venue to
start his UK Tour. Thankfully, for those who managed to get
tickets, this was going to be a memorable show.

I later found out that there had been over 30,000 applications
for tickets making these three gigs the most oversubscribed on
the tour. My tickets were row F in the front stalls — great seats
I thought. Much to my delight, rows A through D had been
removed to accommodate the huge stage, so we ended up in the
second row!

The back of the stage looked similar to the 1976 tour with a
"cage" of strip lights, but this time with colored lamps. The effect
was impressive. The show was mesmerizing, especially the slower
songs from *Low* and *Heroes*. To be so close was amazing — Bowie
had changed his 'look' yet again. This time he seemed healthy and
natural and he didn't appear to be acting out a new character. This
was Bowie playing Bowie. Ghosts of previous incarnations often
appeared with tracks from Ziggy and Station to Station, however
they were given new interpretations which the audience loved.

The oddest part of the show was the interval. Being an old
theatre, the minute Bowie left the stage and the house lights came

up, two elderly ladies appeared at the bottom of each aisle in the stalls selling ice cream. How fantastic — Bowie and a choc-ice! Happy Days!!!

The show was divided into two sections, the first being songs mainly consisting of material from *Low* and *Heroes*, and the second tracks from *Ziggy Stardust* and *Station to Station*. The end was a powerful rendition of "Rebel Rebel" as the final encore and we left to catch the midnight express home. A great night.

Three Nights on the Farm — Stafford Bingley Hall – 24, 25 and 26 June 1978

We had booked a bed and breakfast at a farm not too far from Stafford, which, yet again, proved to be a strange choice of venue. The hall was located on the site of the Staffordshire County Showground which seemed more suited to agricultural events than rock and roll.

The venue was huge and cavernous — the complete opposite of the intimate and cozy hall in Newcastle. No ice cream in the interval here! These gigs were unseated so it meant you could get to the front of the stage quite easily. The biggest surprise was that several of the band members would wander among the audience before the shows started. I'd recognized Carlos Alomar on the first night and I made sure I had a pen handy for the second night. He was an incredibly friendly guy and was happy to autograph my ticket. George Murray and Dennis Davis were also spotted.

The crowds were really enthusiastic on all three nights, yet very well behaved. Many were still dressed in flamboyant outfits inspired by Bowie's past, despite having to trek across fields and join long queues before getting in. Those who were copying Bowie's latest persona sporting a simple check shirt, blue jeans and hiking boots were able to fare better with this converted cattle market! The shows were still amazing. I think the spectacular use of the lighting worked well in the larger venues and the sound was unexpectedly good. Simon House on electric violin added such a unique and distinctive quality.

It was at these shows that I realized Bowie had been incredibly clever in balancing the set list. The dark slow songs from *Low* and *Heroes* were always followed by a fast tempo number, almost as a reward for the audience's patience. We had noticed several huge cameras and a film crew at all three gigs. I guessed that a film was intended for later release. I believe we saw the same at the Earl's Court shows.

Staying on a farm was a great idea. Each night we'd drive back being careful not to make too much noise. We were in a self-contained cottage next to the main house, but we didn't want to wake up the chickens! Our three day break in the country was over far too quickly, but we still had Earl's Court to look forward to.

Earl's Court – 29, 30 June and 1 July 1978

These gigs felt totally different compared to those in Stafford or Newcastle. I think that because this was London and Bowie's home town there was an excitement in the air unlike any of the other venues.

Our seats on the first night were front row (or so we thought). As we approached the front of the stage we could see a mysterious "extra" row had been added in and we'd become the second row. It is difficult to complain when you are that close to the stage anyway. The extra row seemed allocated to various VIPs who arrived only five minutes before the lights dimmed. Someone said they'd seen Dustin Hoffman wandering around.

The only other time Bowie had played Earl's Court was in 1973 where poor sound had virtually led to a mini riot — but there were no issues this time around. The sound was crystal clear and Bowie delivered three superb shows.

The final gig on July 1st was my last chance to see the show on this tour. I'd managed to get six tickets for friends and work colleagues. It was a Saturday night so everybody wanted to go! Mike, Debbie, Alison, Sue and Sue's mate Maureen and I all took our seats ready for the performance to begin.

It was a far more rowdy and enthusiastic audience, so much so that we were all standing on our seats for most of the concert, although a lot of fans from further back tried to muscle in by tunneling under the seats! It was more like a mosh pit in those front few rows, but it was still fun and good natured. The whole place erupted when Bowie announced he would perform "Sound and Vision" as a special "last night treat" for all of us. The show was over and the house lights came up. We climbed back down to earth and made our way back home.

The tour was over for us and it had been fantastic. We didn't know at the time, but it would be another five years before we would get the chance to see Bowie again.

MY FANTASTIC VOYAGE

Denise Heptinstall, UK

 ℐ'D ALWAYS BEEN AWARE of hits like "Space Oddity," "Life on Mars," and "The Jean Genie" when I was growing up, but the first time I really became aware of David Bowie was in the summer of 1980 when I first heard "Ashes to Ashes" on the radio. I was on holiday in Wales with my family and was fascinated by its strangeness every time I heard it: the odd arrangements of the music and Bowie's high voice. "Do you remember a guy that's been…"

The following year, 1981, my dad died and everything was suddenly very different. I was 15 years old and during those summer holidays my best friend and I bought the album *The Best of Bowie*. I was fascinated by Bowie's face on the cover with two different colored eyes. I brought the album home and played it again and again. I realized I did know most of the songs on the album, but I was blown away by the songs that I didn't know like "Diamond Dogs," "Breaking Glass," and "Rock n' Roll Suicide." I loved "Breaking Glass" and its great line, "You're such a wonderful person, but you've got problems." Listening to that album was the start of something very big.

From then on I would go out most Saturdays and buy a Bowie Album. Sometimes I'd go to Camden Lock Market and buy a bootleg tape from two New Romantic guys who had a record stall there. At the end of 1981, *The Man Who Fell to Earth* was shown on TV. I fell in love with Thomas Jerome Newton and his delicate otherworldly looks. It was, and still is, my favorite film of all time. A couple of my friends got a *Man Who Fell to Earth* haircut. I always wanted a "Ziggy" haircut, but my hair was too wavy.

The fanzine *Starzone* also came out around this time and I used to look forward to every issue. I collected each one. We also came across *Bowie Scribes*, a fanzine for pen pals to connect. We made some good friends and sometimes we would meet up in London or go visit them. When we went into London there was always the excitement of maybe meeting our idol in town! At school, we used to write Bowie lyrics all over our exercise books and I had a huge cartoon drawing of Ziggy Stardust inside my desk.

There was always a Bowie album and song to suit my mood and his music always had the ability to make you feel like he knows exactly how you are feeling. After about eighteen months, it was announced at the beginning of 1983 that there would be a new Bowie album and tour. We had eighth row seats in front of the stage at Wembley Arena. Hearing the announcer say, "For the first time in five years, David Bowie and his band!" and seeing my hero saunter on stage in his bright yellow suit to the opening strains of "The Jean Genie" was a dream come true! At one instance, Bowie pointed straight at me and smiled!

The second concert I went to that year was at the huge Milton Keynes Bowl in July. I was there early in the morning and waited hours in the queue, then ran as fast as I could and reached the second row! It was a hot, magical day and a wonderful concert that had a festival feel due to the huge number of people.

Also in 1983 there was a Bowie convention in London. There was a lookalike competition with an amazing Ziggy Stardust winner who could do all the moves. Bowie's manager from the sixties, Ken Pitt, was also there signing autographs. Later, I went to see Lindsay Kemp perform at a theater in London and waited backstage to meet him and get an autograph.

In 1997 I saw Bowie's appearance on the Jack Docherty show in London where he did a really funny interview. I was also lucky enough to get a ticket for the Hanover Grand, a 500 capacity club in London. It was great seeing Bowie in such a small venue and also do a drum and bass set.

I'd been to see Bowie's headlining appearance at the Phoenix Festival in 1996, and was really pleased when it was announced that he would be headlining again in 1997. He played a drum and bass set under the name Tao Jones Index in the dance tent on Saturday night before his main stage appearance on Sunday. I didn't know much about dance music, so for me it was a new experience being in a crowded dance tent listening to the fantastic Bentley Rhythm Ace! For Bowie's main stage appearance on Sunday, I arrived early and met a sixteen year old boy who had travelled from Israel as well as a girl from France. She had been inspired to learn English so she could understand Bowie's lyrics, which in turn led her to become an English teacher! I was in the middle, front row that concert — directly in front of the microphone. It was magical when Bowie came on stage with his guitar and started singing "Quicksand." I think it is my favorite Bowie concert.

I went on an organized coach trip to France to see Bowie in Lyons and Antibes, saw a concert in Liverpool and then the two great shows at Shepherds Bush Empire which finished off the European tour. It was such a lovely atmosphere queuing up all day outside with fans that had been on the coach trip as well as others who had come from all over Europe. I remember a group of German school teachers who had Bowie's autograph tattooed on their arms!

For the London Astoria concert in 1999 I foolishly decided to swap my tickets for standing tickets by paying extra to a ticket tout!

I realized too late that they were forgeries, but amazingly a fan that was not able to attend came along and gave me his standing tickets. The shows "stand out moment" was when David put on a feather boa that someone had thrown on stage and sang "Drive in Saturday." The last time I saw Bowie in concert was at the Isle of Wright Festival in 2004 my last front row. It was amazing.

In 2013 I was happy and surprised when *The Next Day* was released and I loved the album. I went to see the "David Bowie Is" exhibition twice at the Victoria and Albert Museum. My favorite exhibits were the letter he wrote in the 1960s replying to a fan, his story boards and hand written lyrics, his cocaine spoon and all of the costumes.

I first listened to *Blackstar* the evening before the news that Bowie had died. Although I think it is fantastic, I still find it hard to listen to. Over the years, I was able to see Bowie 29 times and I have great memories. His music is timeless. Thank you, David.

MY DATE WITH BOWIE

Jasmine Storm, UK

$\mathcal{I}$ WAS RATHER LATE COMING to the party. When David Bowie sang "Starman" to the *Top of the Pops* audience in 1972 I was completely unaware of what this show was. When "Space Oddity" reached number one, I vaguely remember Pans People dancing to it, but as a pre-teen my life was covered in tartan from the Bay City Rollers. However, starting secondary school in 1979 gave me a greater understanding of Bowie's music, and I began to realise what a legend he is. I bought my first album, *Ziggy Stardust*, from a boy in my class for £1.50 which was quite a lot of money to me back then. I fell head over heels in love. It was the start of a love affair that has continued throughout my life.

After *Ziggy*, I bought all the albums I could get my hands on with my limited budget from a paper round and Saturday job in Woolworths. I discovered the early Deram 60s Bowie and rocking glam 70s Bowie and loved it all. And, although it's fair to say I liked some of *Scary Monsters*, I was very much stuck in the 70s. I spent hours listening over and over again to the brilliance of his words and music. I marveled at how clever "Five Years" was and was intrigued at the cut-up technique used on "Moonage Daydream." I fell in love with *Young Americans* and hoped one day to meet someone who would make me feel the way this album did. No other band or musician really ever came close, although I did have a soft spot for Abba.

In 1983 all of my dreams came true. I couldn't believe that not only was Bowie touring, but he was coming to my town! I may have been born in London, but I no longer lived in a big city so for Milton Keynes to be put on the map in this way was more than luck to me — it was fate. No matter what, I would be there!

It wasn't easy to find people who loved Bowie like I did and that would want to go to the concert. Because the gig was local, a couple of school friends came with me. As I was still at school and just had a Saturday job, I could only afford one ticket. It was for the first night, Friday. A good friend offered me his ticket for the Sunday show so I was then able to go twice. Plans to meet in the pub on Saturday to discuss all things Bowie meant the whole weekend would be a Bowie fest!

That Friday morning I got up early and caught a bus to The National Bowl. I had never been there before and I was too young to drive, but I was first in line at 11 am. The doors didn't open until 2 pm and I knew Bowie wouldn't be on until much later, but nothing could dampen my enthusiasm.

I knew we couldn't bring in water or food, so I didn't. I did hide my 110 compact camera in my bag as I really wanted a couple of photographs of Bowie. I knew cameras were not allowed, but I was willing to take the risk. Once inside I ran to the front and secured my space. I had already lost my friends from school, but I didn't care. The sun was shining and I got chatting to a few people around me but no one seemed to love Bowie like I did. I wanted to find someone who knew the album songs — not just the singles. But the people around me didn't talk that way. So I sat in the huge field with the sun shining down and listened to the music from the speakers. This was a perfect day.

I sat through several groups perform but I couldn't wait for Bowie to come on stage! The crowd kept getting sprayed with water as they didn't want anyone to overheat, but I didn't want my mascara to run either!

Eventually it was time. I was so excited, I had butterflies in my stomach and the anticipation was tantalizing. Bowie came on stage and what a vision he was. I was in shock. Blond, a healthy looking tan and a smart suit right in front of me by only a few feet. I couldn't believe it. I felt very emotional and had tears in my eyes. I wanted to capture and breathe in every moment. I was transfixed. We sang along. We danced. When he performed "Cracked Actor" I looked around and found a girl near me who knew the song! We sang it loudly while the rest of the crowd seemed to wait for another song they knew.

I wanted to stop time. I wanted to never let the moment end. There was free shuttle service to the City Centre. I got on and someone asked, "What happened to you?" I replied, "I was at the front!" I was in a daze, clutching my programme that had been a bit damaged, but that didn't matter. I had been at the front and had seen Bowie. Only 48 hours until the next time. Best night of my life? Absolutely!

Years later, my mum was trying to understand my love of Bowie and said to me, "Well if you love him why didn't you marry him?" I said to her, "Mum — he didn't ask me!"

SERIOUS MOONLIGHT, WONDERFUL MEMORIES

Ruth Davison, UK

FIRST SAW DAVID IN concert on 2 July 1983 during the Serious Moonlight tour at Milton Keynes Bowl, England. A boiling hot day in a place I'd never been to before. Excitement was off the scale even before David hit the stage! When he did emerge, the crowd roared and surged and my view was blocked. As I'm just over five feet tall, I remember screaming to my friend, "I can't see him, Janice!" A tall guy in front of me turned and said he'd lift me up so I could see. Though I was a bit scared, I let him lift me and of course got a wonderful view of David for the rest of the first song and the next one! Back on terra firma, the crowd had parted a bit and I now had a clear view through to David on the stage. As the show went on, we edged forward until we were about ten rows from the stage – close enough! I'll never forget how it felt, seeing David live for the first time.

Years later, I was looking through a book about David and found a picture taken with the back of David and the front of the crowd. I could see myself — age 22, arms raised, singing my heart out!

Serious moonlight, wonderful memories!

FIVE YEARS

Petter M. Ness (aka Bewlay), Norway

Five years that really mattered in the life of this Bowie fan:

1983

*T*HE YEAR I FIRST noticed the name David Bowie. Yeah, I know, wrong decade and all that, but give me a break — I was 10! Besides, if you're one of the people who think his best work was behind him, then shame on you. Not that 1983 was *great*, but it had *Let's Dance*. Satellite TV had arrived in Norway and with it music videos. Lots and lots of music videos. And this 10 year old started to notice. Among them were David Bowie crooning under an Australian desert heat about putting on red shoes, dancing the blues and swaying through the crowd to an empty place. I loved it, and I'll love it till the day I die. My friend had an older sister who owned the *Let's Dance* LP. We borrowed it, without permission, time and time again. And that, as they say, was the beginning.

1990

It should have been a great year. After all, David Bowie was doing the Sound & Vision tour and was playing Oslo for the first time since 1978. August 22, 1990 — that was the date of my first ever Bowie gig. I was excited. I had bought the double vinyl edition of *Changesbowie* just to warm up with all the essential hits that he would be playing for his "farewell tour" of all the old favourites.

Like I said, it should have been a great year. But then my father suddenly died, just four weeks before the concert.

Things get put in perspective. You're 17 years old and a coming rock concert is the *biggest thing* ever. But does it really matter in the face of personal tragedy and sorrow?

Yes. Because music matters. Whether a symphony or a simple verse, it can reach you and make you listen and feel even when life seems at its bleakest. For that reason alone, I'm forever grateful to David Bowie for that night in August 1990.

He was a hero, and not just for one day.

1995

I'm staying in London and enjoying the days with my current girlfriend and friends. Watching Spurs play football, having a pint and shooting pool at the Finsbury Park Tavern. Then Bowie releases a new album — *1. Outside*. I head over to Tower Records on the first day of release. It's the maddest thing he's ever done. Absolutely bonkers. A concept album about ritual murders, social outcasts and an artist who makes murder into art. All set in the future. A lad insane, indeed.

Deranged.

I loved it.

Lying on the couch, headphones on, listening to Mike Garson go berserk on the piano on "A Small Plot of Land." Thinking that being a Bowie fan was truly *exciting* again, and not for the things he had done — but for what lay ahead.

So what if volumes 2, 3, 4, and 5 never happened? We got

this one. The concept and execution was frequently panned and ridiculed by critics. Poor souls — they didn't know what hit them. Today its greatness is widely recognized.

1997

Skip ahead two years. I won't dwell on *Earthling*, but man, that tour! I caught three gigs that summer. Starting out with the wettest gig I've ever been to — at the Kalvoya Festival outside Oslo. The rain is pouring down. We're all drenched — even the men and women on the stage. David shakes his fist at the sky and shouts: "Go ahead — do your worst!" But we all enjoyed every minute.

Six weeks later and I'm in Glasgow, heading down to the Barrowlands and politely trying to explain to a group of Glasgow Rangers supporters that I'll be fine on my own walking through "Celtic land" on my way to the venue (thinking that 20 blue shirts will more likely cause trouble than just a lone soul on his way to a Bowie gig).

The day after, I'm on a bus towards Manchester to catch my second gig in as many nights. I was able to see them because of that nifty invention called The Internet. In 1997 I was making friends all over the world — and they were getting me tickets. Thanks, *Teenage Wildlife* Message board. And thanks Jeaj, Alys, Kaliman, RaMoana and many others for being part of my life 20 years later. Oh, and Bowie turned 50 and had the greatest birthday bash ever!

2016

Yes, I know it sucked! Big time. Nearly a year later and it still hurts. I'll remember where I was and what I was doing on *that* horrible day for the rest of my life. So why bring it up? Because, as The Observers on *Fringe* would say, it was important.

Back in 1990 I had to learn the hard way that life goes on.

One of the people who helped me get through a rough time was David Bowie. That summer event, that music, was what I needed at the time.

On 8 January 2016 Bowie turned 69. His latest album, *Blackstar*, arrived in my mailbox that very day. It was Friday; I was working from home so I put it on. I listened to it again and again throughout that weekend, thinking: "He'd done it again!" That brilliant, brilliant man! It was unlike anything he'd ever made — and it was great. Truly, truly great.

The following Monday, on my way to work, I made the mistake of checking the news. The rest of that day went by in a haze. As he sings on "Girl Loves Me": "Where the f★★★ did Monday go?!" I remember sitting in my chair that evening, listening to *Blackstar* again, and as the last track neared its end it suddenly dawned on me: "This is it. This is the last thing he'll ever do." And I wept.

Thanks for everything, Major Tom. You may be strung out in heaven high, while the rest of us are hitting all-time lows, but know that we're grateful to you for blowing our minds.

WAITING FOR THE MAN

John Davey, Ireland

 $\mathcal{J}$ T ALL STARTED FOR me in 1976. I had seen Bowie sing "Golden Years" on *Top of the Pops* and thought how cool he looked — good song too. I remembered back when as a kid I had seen him perform "Starman" with his arm draped around Mick Ronson. I bought *Hunky Dory* in 1976 and became instantly hooked.

I was ecstatic when it was announced he was playing Slane. I had travelled to London in 1978 at age 16 to see Bowie at Earl's Court. This gained me a Bowie cult status at school. A few years later, in 1983, my best mate from school and I travelled with our girlfriends to see Bowie. Now he was playing practically on my doorstep. I passed Slane Castle everyday on the way to work. I had a plan.

Lord Henry Mountcharles owns Slane Castle. He is known as being a bit of a cool cat when it comes to things musical. Guys I worked with who lived in Slane and knew him said he was an eccentric, but a genuinely nice guy. It was quite simple, a genial plan that couldn't fail — write to Lord Mountcharles, tell him how big a fan I was, enclose the '78 ticket stub and picture of me outside K. WEST and I'd get to meet David Bowie backstage! I waited and waited for the reply. No reply. Dammit, why didn't I send a stamped addressed envelope? At least I would have gotten my precious ticket stub back. Then one Saturday, on the way home from work, Lord Mountcharles passed me in his green Mercedes. I turned and followed him through the gates and up to his front door.

"Lord Henry, I'm sorry to intrude but I wrote to you about David Bowie. I sent you a photo of myself posing as Ziggy outside K. WEST and…"

"Ah yes, I remember the letter. I'm sorry but I've been so busy I didn't get to reply to you." To cut a long conversation short, not even he could pull strings to get me a meeting with David Bowie because of security and all that. So I thanked him for bringing Bowie to Slane and left — utterly despondent and deflated.

The next day a very small piece in the *Sunday World* newspaper announced a coup for Ryanair. Ann O'Callaghan, PR for Ryanair, stated that Bowie would use Ryanair to fly into Dublin for the concert at Slane. I had another plan.

I called Ryanair and asked to speak to Ms. Ann O'Callaghan. I explained who I was, how much I loved David Bowie's music and what it meant to me, and well…if she could just tell me what day and time he was flying into Dublin Airport I could take it from there. Of course she told me she couldn't possibly give out that kind of information, but ring her back later that afternoon. I did, and she just said, "John, 4 o' clock Thursday afternoon — good luck." God bless that woman — she passed away tragically with cancer a few years later — a beautiful kind woman.

I had finished working my third and final night shift and was getting into bed for a few hours' sleep. I told Caroline, my wife, to waken me at 12 because I wanted to be at the airport at 2 o'clock. She looked at me bemused, but smiled because she knew what it meant to me.

I walked into the airport terminal and looked around for a while. Then I spotted a TV crew from RTE, the state broadcaster. I went over and asked if they knew where Bowie would emerge from, the time he was arriving, etc. It turned out I knew more about his arrival than they did. The guy who was to interview him asked me about his entourage, his latest album and so on. I walked with them as they arrived at a door. "I'm sorry but we have to go inside now to the press room — the media guys are interviewing him after we have done our piece — good luck with your autograph hunt." As the door opened and they were greeted, I looked at him and said "can I come in with you guys?" He looked at me, thinking, and said "Come on!" I was in the press conference as part of a TV crew with all the press reporters waiting for David Bowie!!

Inside the guy said, "We might get you to chat with him and film you getting your LP signed — just stay in the background and don't attract any attention to yourself until I give you the nod." One of the press guys came over to me and said, "I see you have his latest album, you must be a big fan. What newspaper are you writing for?" When I told him how I had got into the press room and who I was he just said "cool" and smiled and told me to wait. Then about six other press guys came over and said, "You're a fan right? Tell us about him, who is Coco Schwab? What's his best LP? Why did he kill Ziggy?"

Then disaster. An announcer at the top table said, "Gentlemen of the press, regretfully Mr. Bowie has had to cancel this press conference — we're sorry for this inconvenience to you all." There were angry exchanges and threats of the media refusing to cover his arrival at all The TV guy came over to me and said "we're going out in a people carrier to meet him on the tarmac and do the interview as we travel back to the terminal. I'm sorry but this is as far as you can go. I really hope you get his autograph, sorry."

So close, but so far. My hopes seemed dashed. Then the press guys came over to me. "John, isn't it? We need you to do something. Bowie is going to come through the arrivals door just like any other passenger. He is going to have his own security guys with him. Your job is to stop him, get him talking, get him to sign your LP and give us plenty of time to get some decent shots of him. Don't forget to look up at us and try and tell him about how you got in here — we'll call your name so he'll know you've been talking with us. That way he'll look at the cameras and give us some shots. Did you get all of that?"

"Err...yes, of course. Can I ask you guys a favor in return? Is it possible to get copies of your photos of him and me together?" So the deal was struck — the following Monday I was to go to the offices of the *Irish Press, Irish Independent* and *Irish Times* to collect the photos.

When Bowie walked through the doors, I walked straight up to him and said "Hello David, welcome to Ireland. I've been a fan for many years since I was a kid, can you sign my LP..." then his security guy sneakily caught the top of my pocket and yanked me out of the way and David Bowie moved on. When I looked at the LP, the autograph had already smudged and because it was a shiny cover the marker pen he had used really didn't come out to well. So I ducked around the crowd, through the press photographers and said, "David, sorry but can you sign it again with my pen — the first one didn't come out too good." He stopped and smiled, "Sure." He said. Then a girl gave him a rose and asked "can I have a kiss?" He kissed her on the cheek! Then he gave me back my LP and my pen and said, "Enjoy the concert young man," and he exited the terminal. He got into the back of a Mercedes limo with the window down and as it pulled away I said "all the best for Saturday David" and he smiled and waved goodbye to me.

The press guys came over and congratulated me on getting his autograph. They took pictures of me holding the LP over my head. They wanted to know what he had said to me, what I had said to him, was it a thrill to meet my hero. I had rehearsed this answer the night before at work as I knew it would guarantee me a mention in the paper. "For almost everyone in Ireland they'll remember the Pope coming to visit, for me it will be the day I met David Bowie."

That evening, in the final editions of the *Evening Press*, David Bowie and I appeared on the front page. The next morning the story was on the front of the three main national newspapers. Most important though, I had met Bowie and had his autograph!

All my mates couldn't believe the story until they had read it in the papers. I was called "The hard neck Davey" as described in the *Independent*. On the way into the gig, a guy and his girlfriend stopped me and said, "You're him — you're the guy who met Bowie." The gig was class, even if the weather was a bit damp.

So that's my Bowie story...almost...

I had found out that Bowie was staying in the Westbury Hotel in Dublin — he was spotted walking on Grafton Street and had gone back to the hotel. So after I picked up my photos (where I met Miss Ireland, Collette Jackson, in a lift in the Irish Press Building. She too was collecting photographs. "Hello Miss Ireland, how are you? You are very pretty, congratulations on winning." "Thank you. Aren't you the guy who met Bowie at the airport?") I headed over to the Westbury Hotel.

"Oh no. Not this time!" It was his security man. I showed him the photographs. "Gee, they're pretty good." Said the security guy. "I couldn't stop you from getting to talk to him. You were pretty persistent. You won't see him this time though, he's leaving from the basement car park. The band are in the lounge though!"

I watched Carlos Alomar come down a flight of stairs. "Carlos, will you autograph my picture?" When he saw the picture he remarked how good it looked and then brought me into the lounge and introduced me to the band including Peter Frampton and Carmine Rojas. They all autographed my photo. Carlos was great, chatting to me about Bowie and how they worked when recording and gigging. He was his band leader. I had a coffee with him! Then they all boarded a bus and I waved them off as they headed for the airport and the next gig.

When I showed my wife and my mates the photos in the pub that night, they couldn't believe the pictures or the autographs of the band. My mate who had been to Milton Keynes with me in '83 looked at me and said, "Andy Warhol must have been right — everyone will be famous for 15 minutes!" I just looked at him and said: "It's War-hole actually, you said Hull, it's Hole...as in Holes." The two of us burst out laughing and got drunk and sang "Starman."

And that's how I met Mr. David Jones aka Ziggy Stardust aka Aladdin Sane aka Thomas Jerome Newton aka David Bowie.

A TOUR OF THE STADIUM
Patti Brett, USA

On 1987, DURING THE Glass Spider Tour, my friend Carlin and I decided to travel to Canada to see David Bowie. We were friends with Carlos Alomar, David's musical director/guitarist and he let us know in which hotel he was staying. We were trying to make plans to meet up prior to the show, but Carlos told us he had to go to the sound check. We told him we would catch up with him later.

Disappointed, we were trying to figure out what to do with our afternoon when I remembered the venue, Olympic Stadium, offered tours of the facility. We decided to go to the venue, take a tour and see if we could get into the sound check.

We drove to the stadium and signed up for a tour that, thankfully, was leaving in just a few minutes. We could not believe our luck when we walked into the building and heard the band playing. We needed to ditch the tour group. But how? The tour guide was talking about the structure being built for the 1976 Olympics. All we were hearing was "blah, blah, blah." We were so close, but so far, from our goal. At this point we were desperate to get away from the group. The guide said there was a show that night and we were hearing the sound check. Carlin and I told the tour guide we needed to use the restroom, and she pointed us in

the direction of the ladies. We ran off and went in the restroom
frantic to break free from the group. Finally, we resigned ourselves
to the fact that we would have to wait until we were further along
on the tour to try and get away. When we left the ladies room the
group was standing at the top of one of the aisles and our guide
said that they were just listening to the sound check. I confessed
that was the reason we were there, not for the tour, and the guide
wished us well!

Carlin decided she really did need to use the restroom, so I
told her I would wait at the top of one of the aisles where I could
look down at the stage. But David was right there. I couldn't be
that far away. I ran down the steps and stood on the right side of
the stage. The band started to check "Loving The Alien" which
is one of my favorite Bowie songs. David saw me standing on the
side of the stage and walked over while he was singing. When he
got to the chorus, he smiled, fell to his knees and started singing
the song to me! I was in tears. He stayed there for the duration of
the song and Carlin came down the steps, just as he finished. It
was a moment I will never forget.

We stayed until the sound check was over. I think we saw them
perform six songs in total. It was like our own private concert.
We didn't get to see Carlos until we got back to the hotel. What
a great experience!

THOSE FLYING MACHINES

Dale K. Perry, USA

THE CALL CAME ON a hot summer night in 1991 when I least expected it. Did I want to fly to Los Angeles for a private Tin Machine performance? Did I? Is there any answer except "yes" to a question like that? Forget that I'd been pretending to be a responsible adult for quite some time, forget that I had a career with schedules to maintain, forget that I'm on the east coast and will need to fly to the west coast, stay in a hotel, and all the other incidental costs I wasn't planning for. Do I want to go to LA to see Tin Machine? You betcha!

Of course, Tin Machine in itself is a tough sell. I'm hard pressed to find anyone especially thrilled about this incarnation of David Bowie and many hoped it was over after the first album release and performances. The Sales brothers along with a guitar player from New England are the band? Bowie is simply the lead singer? And no music from *Ziggy Stardust* or *Young Americans*? No big production like the Glass Spider Tour? No worries. Let's face it, David Bowie could sit on a stage and read the telephone book out loud and I'd be happy to attend.

The particulars of explaining, but not really, why I was going away for a few (four to be exact) days and my walking on air mood took me through the next couple of weeks. During the 1990

Sound and Vision tour I had come to the conclusion that the next Bowie show I attended I would be located within 50 feet of the stage or I simply wasn't going. I was finished with sitting a football field away or so far up in the air that I pulled every muscle in my body walking up the stairs to get to the seat. Since the mid-1970s I was thrilled to attend any show I could, but enough was enough. This LA opportunity — linked to a Sound and Vision fan meet up (thanks to Julie of the *Sound and Vision* Fanzine) — seemed like a chance to be someplace smaller than a stadium and just mysterious enough to override any hesitation about travel issues.

As it turned out, most of the fans who traveled to LA stayed in the same hotel — and we were a group from around the world that was beyond excited to be unexpectedly gathered for this event. I'm not sure if it's my failing memory or I really did not know at the time, but even once in LA it seemed we were not aware of the location for the Tin Machine show; we only knew that it was a Sunday evening event and a bus would pick us up at the hotel. We lined up, got on the bus and it takes off heading to the only other place I've ever been in California — LAX Airport! That was where we were headed — for a taping of the ABC television *In Concert* series that was to be filmed in the outdoor cargo area of LAX airport!

If you can, just imagine: jets flying overhead, lots of noise, a bunch (250?) of David Bowie — and maybe one or two Tin Machine — fans and a small fenced in area behind a large hanger. There was a stage set up, the runway was well in the distance behind the stage and you could see airplanes taking off and landing. We walked about talking amongst ourselves although other people were already there when we arrived. This was also a press event. Some attendees looked bored; clearly it was a "requirement" for them to be there. The cameras and individuals responsible for filming were setting up and I was thrilled to be in such a small area. I spent a few moments trying to decide if I wanted to be close to the stage or farther back so I could see both the stage and the backdrop of flying aircraft at the same time. I walked into a maze of people and then moved off to the side where I wouldn't get knocked over. When I looked up, there was this faintly familiar looking man in a shockingly bright green suit standing directly in front of me. David Bowie. I know I gasped and I know he smiled. And I know I don't remember anything else except I was eventually about the equivalent of four rows from the stage for my first Tin Machine show. It was an incredible experience — the music, David Bowie and those jets taking off and landing during the concert. Over too soon, but wasn't it always?

That trip to Los Angeles began a four month whirlwind of seeing the Tin Machine "It's My Life" tour in several different cities. I finally wasn't being seated in (literally) left field. I had front row seats at The Tower in Philadelphia – truly a dream come true. More importantly, I met some very wonderful people who became lifelong friends.

Whether you liked Tin Machine or not, there is no disputing that in 1991 David Bowie never looked healthier, happier or sexier.

Delicious.

DO YOU REMEMBER ME?

Marla Kanevsky, USA

On October 1997, WXPN had arranged a fundraiser at the iconic Sigma Sound Studios in Philadelphia. It was to be an acoustic show featuring Reeves Gabrels and, of course, David Bowie. The tickets were $1,000 for two. That was out of the question for me. However, we wanted to try to see David as he arrived for the show, and knew how wonderful it would be to see him outside of Sigma, 23 years after the Young Americans sessions and listening party. So off we went to hang out at the studio.

In addition to myself, our group included fellow Sigma Kid Leslie, my then nine year old son Zane, and Zane's dad. Several others, including Sigma Kid Patti were on their way back to Philly from a Bowie show in Boston. The four of us arrived fairly early in the morning to begin our vigil. Zane was dressed in leather pants and a spectacular, shiny, silver lame shirt. Pretty snazzy!

Not to be disappointed, several hours later a white van pulled up. David emerged from the van and walked directly towards Zane who was eager to meet David again. Zane asked, "Hello David. Do you remember me?" David replied, "Of course…Zane, how are you?" David stopped for a photograph or two and Zane took that opportunity to hand David a fan letter that he had written to him. I had the original photo of Patti, David, Luther and I taken by Dagmar back in 1974 and David graciously autographed it for me and got a kick out of the ongoing Sigma connection.

I remember saying something about not being able to get tickets for the show. David apologized, hugged me and said, "I'm sorry love, it's not my gig." I took that as meaning he had no control over the cost of the tickets, etc. But wow! So we got ready to settle in for the several hour wait so that we could see David again later when he would be leaving the show.

Not more than five minutes passed, the door to the studio opened and someone leaned out motioning for Zane to come over. He said to Zane, "Bring your parents in…David would like to invite you as his special guests!" They kindly also invited Leslie in — Zane's "Aunt Leslie."

Here we were again, living a once in a lifetime experience, in Philly, at Sigma and with David Bowie! I'm guessing that once inside David read Zane's fan letter and, being the amazing man he was, took it to the next level, again! During the show there were a couple of times that David spoke to Zane, one time thanking him for carrying on the tradition of wearing shiny clothes! Another time, singing the line *Zane, Zane, Zane* from "All the Madmen." Unfortunately, I believe all the parts of the show that included audience participation were cut.

My favorite picture — perhaps of all time — is the one where Zane is beaming while handing David his fan letter. Zane's face says it all.

"FOR SIMONE..."
Simone Metge, Germany

$\mathcal{O}$N JUNE 2000, I arrived in New York two days before the first Roseland show. Thanks to another BowieNetter, we knew where David was rehearsing for the concerts and right after my arrival we went to wait for him to come out. He looked pretty tired and scruffy, so we only said "hello." I had come with only a backpack, but in it I had a stuffed animal as a gift for the yet-to-be-born Lexi. So I said to David, "Here, this is for you. I don't want to carry it around any longer." He took the stuffed animal and replied with a grin, "Aahh, I see. So now you want me to carry it around instead?" Haha! Yup, that was the plan! He thanked me with a kiss on the cheek.

That evening I wrote him a lengthy email about how much I loved New York (which I didn't the first time I was there in 1995). Thanks to Bnet, I was able to exchange several emails with David for a while which I will always treasure. I also told him I'd be back the next day where he was rehearsing, even though I'd be very embarrassed. I finished the email quite cheeky with the words: "P.S. You are looking great, but I hope you shave again before Friday."

So just as I had promised (or threatened?), the next morning I went back to the rehearsal studio and waited for him. It didn't take long until he came strolling along the street. I was nervous. I felt like hiding behind a tiny tree on the curb! David smiled, said "hi," shook my hand and asked how long I had been there. He also asked, "So that other girl is picking you up?" I didn't understand him, and he repeated it. I still didn't get it, so he rephrased it and asked "So you are staying with that other girl?" I was stunned. It was something I mentioned in my email to him. That was the proof that he really read them! Wonderful!

I was wearing a black shirt on which I decided to have all Bowienetters write their name and so I asked David if he could sign it. He asked if he should do it really nicely, with "For Simone?" Whoohoo, he actually remembered my name! "No," I said, "just sign it with "Sailor" and he did with a smirk.

I also had a nice picture from a magazine with me, which I asked him to sign and yes, now with "For Simone" please. So he thought a second and then wrote, "For Simone, with love, Bowie 2000." Even though I got quite a few autographs over the years, this one remains my favorite. I thanked him with a kiss on the cheek. He returned the kiss and then went inside. I floated away to meet some friends.

Later that day I noticed his email reply, which he had sent the previous night. "Simone, promise to shave. Sailor." What a lovely day!

ABSOLUTE CHATTERS
RaMoana, USA

$\mathcal{O}$N THE NEW DAYS of the World Wide Web and computer ownership, most of my Bowie interaction was online. Back in the days of *TeenageWildlife*, the Chat was the place to go. I called it my "pad" as I was there nearly 24/7. Sometimes Bowie's son Duncan dropped in as "Dunbeetle" or something "Dun" and would play with us (once he said he only came there to find out where his father was — the site had this clever world map of the Earthling Tour.)

I had the feeling sometimes that Bowie was with Duncan, looking over his shoulder or even chatting himself. Bowie could not really type yet — you could tell it was hunt and peck and sometimes wrong when it was Bowie (also in *BowieNet* Chat later). We had moderated chats on *BowieNet*, sometimes with famous guests and I still have some of the chatlogs. Sometimes Bowie would just pop in and be excited to talk about books or music or whatever he was working on, like *Hours*.

Bowie also mentioned *2. Contamination*, and promised it would happen. He also said we would have Debbie Harry as a chat guest. Sometime later, he popped into the chat and everyone was trying to get his attention. I put in all caps: *When Are We Getting 2. Contamination and The Chat With Debbie Harry*? Well, he noticed and said: *Don't Yell R, or I'll Yell Back.* However, he never answered the question!

When Bowie opened *BowieNet* he was like a kid opening a candy store and I'll never forget when they added the davidbowie. com email addresses. I was in *BowieNet* Chat with Bowie at the time and could not find the tab for email! He instructed me on where to find it rather impatiently (I know I was a dork!) and told me to check my email. He knew I would find out how to open it then! Sure enough, he had sent me an email!

THE BIRTHDAY CONCERT
A TALE OF TWO GUESTS
Kali and Belle, USA

$\mathcal{I}$T WAS THE BEST of times, it was the queasiest of times.

The Characters
Belle: An admirer of Mr. Bowie since 1973
Kali: Four months into the David Bowie stuff and still trying to
figure it all out

A Sunday Evening in December

Belle's phone rings…
Kali: So, when do we go see Bowie again? I've really enjoyed
some of the CDs you loaned me.
Belle: Not for a while; you know, sometimes one goes years
and years without attending a live performance. Consider
yourself fortunate, you may get to see a tour in 1997.

The Next Morning at 9:15 am
Kali's office phone rings…

Belle: OK, Kali...sit down. You may want to schedule some vacation time in January — looks like we're going to Mr. Bowie's Birthday party. I already have the tickets!

Kali: Of course I'm sitting down. I'm at work. We're what? You what? You're shittin me! Oh my God! Oh Wow! I can't believe I'm going to another concert so soon. I can't believe it's his *Birthday Concert*! This is unbelievable!

Note: Kali calls Belle a short time later to confirm that this conversation actually took place.

January 7, 1997 (a telephone conversation)

Kali: I guess we're all set. The weather forecast doesn't look too promising, but I do have the train schedules.

Belle: We may be all set, but I have the stomach flu...don't worry, I'll be fine...(?)

January 9, 1997, mid-afternoon

Belle: Here we go. It's snowing, sleeting and freezing rain is coming down, cars are sliding off the highway and my stomach feels like the ocean. I'll be fine....

Kali: Snow and this ice. Fortunate for me that Belle is driving. I mean, how bad is this weather? Besides, aren't pickup trucks supposed to be good in bad weather? We seem to be moving along. Can't wait to get on the train. Gotta love em!

On the Train

Kali: On the train with my Roy Rogers chicken. It's warm here, I have my leg room, what more could I ask for? Isn't this exciting?? She's eating my fries. Oh well, maybe a little food will help her stomach. I love trains!

Belle: The damn train. I hate trains...I mean, how *do* they stay on the tracks? Wish I had known someone who could have airlifted me into the Garden. Why did I eat those French fries? Am I crazy?

Kali: Hmmmm…she's kinda quiet. I'll try some chitchat to take her mind off her stomach.

Maybe I'll tell her about some of the new collections we just got in at work (I'm an archivist). "Hey Belle, did I tell you about the new collection we have on the 1958 Bayonne Train Wreck? It took place not far from where we are now…"

At the Garden

Belle: We made it. I'm still in one piece and the ocean in my stomach has simmered down to a rippling lake. Not a very long line to get inside; fortunately we can wander around, we're not in the mosh pit.

Kali: Damn it's cold here. She must really be ill — she said she wanted a cigarette before we went inside and we got halfway up the stairs when she remembered she forgot to have it! It's nice not having to wait in line, although that line isn't really long. Evan Torrie of *Teenage Wildlife* said he'd be here at 5:00. It's now 6:45 and I don't see him. I wonder if he had trouble getting into NYC because of the weather.

The Doors Open —— Sort Of

Belle: Is anyone coordinating this insane rush through the gate? I again thank myself for getting seats for this event, although Kali may not enjoy the show as much. Oh well, not much sympathy here….it was years before I ever saw Bowie without using binoculars! Kali spent his only two shows standing 5 feet from the stage! Besides, our seats should be good. Maybe we'll just wait out this crazy rush here in the lobby, watching the *Teenage Wildlife* birthday card on the

screen. I really like those posters surrounding the screen...
and what's this? A security sheet for the evening's event?
Hmmmm...this could be a potential souvenir...

Kali: Oh, they're letting them in — into the lobby? That's
it? What was the point of making them wait outside?
Now they are all mashed together with no sense of order
(practice for the pit?) Oh well, might as well go in and keep
warm. This is cool — the *Teenage Wildlife* Birthday Card
is playing on the monitors. Nice posters, too! Wonder if
I could liberate one as a potential souvenir. Ah, no luck.
Well, maybe after the show.

Inside the Garden and Seated

Kali: These are pretty good seats! Damn, forgot to bring my
grandfather's WWII Field Artillery binoculars. Oh well.
Is that a floating eye backstage? There are those suspended
bodies again. I wonder what they signify. Does he have
that St. George icon on stage again? I can't quite see. Oh
look, there's the table! I remember Belle telling me about
that at the club concerts...oh, what song is that for...boy,
the pit is half empty. We should be down there. Where is
everyone? All the seats here are empty! Oh look! I think
that's Evan down there. So, this is Placebo, eh? They're
damn good! Oh no, Belle's getting up. Where is she going?

Belle: These aren't bad seats — I've had better and worse. Have a
great view of the inside of the stage...look, are those eyes
floating about back there? And that seems to be a coat rack.
Placebo has started playing and the arena is empty yet. This
is the best opening band I've heard in a long time! The pit
doesn't look too filled yet either, maybe we should have
gotten tickets there. I'm feeling much better, maybe I'll go
get something to eat.

Kali: She's eating *pizza*?

Belle: Here we go. I can see David and the band making their
        way up the steps onto the stage…"Little Wonder" opens
        the evening, followed by "Hearts Filthy Lesson." So far, I
        think that my favorite from *Earthling* is "Little Wonder,"
        of course I have now heard it a few times. David has on a
        lovely frock coat…I've always been a big fan of frock coats
        (didn't know that frocks had fans, did you?)

Kali: Movement back stage. But I can't quite see who's who —
        ah, there he is! This is great! He's opening with "Little
        Wonder." I love this one! This is my favorite from *Earthling*
        (not that I've heard all that any). "Hearts Filthy Lesson" is
        good, too! I've recognized two songs already! I even know
        the words! Not bad for a fan of only four months! Gotta
        love his frock. Oh look — a coat rack! Wonder if he's got
        that awesome Union Jack frock on there.

Belle: The arena has filled and here's the start of the special
        guests. Well, you must say this for David: absolutely *no
        one* that shares his stage ever comes close to having the
        classic appearance or aura that he does. Even so, special
        guests in particular, couldn't we dress it up just a little
        bit? Kali should be recognizing some of these songs from
        the September club dates. I just can't imagine what he is
        seeing or hearing as he's so new to this ("Scary Monsters;"
        "Fashion").

Kali: This is great! I actually recognize these songs! I'm having
        flashbacks to my first two concerts. Who's that guy singing
        with him. He looks like a stage hand. Geez, at least tuck
        your shirt in!

Belle: Here come the eyes! Interesting effect, although I wish
        they had more staying power. With the exception of one
        eye, they didn't make it any farther than the pit. ("Telling
        Lies"). Time for "Hallo Spaceboy" — I just love the
        moondust coming from the audience, it has such a nice

effect when it shimmers in the lights, yes? ("Seven Years in Tibet;" "The Man Who Sold The World")

Kali: Oh cool! Look at all those eyes! They won't last long though. "Telling Lies" — I think I enjoyed this better the first time I heard it in Philly, but it's not bad. I really like this next song, but I don't remember the name of it. Man, that drummer is really getting into it — he looks like Animal from the Muppets! What's with the glitter and the cards? They did this at the other concerts, too!

Belle: Wonder if we'll sing Happy Birthday? Ah, now here's a hairstyle if I've ever seen one — Robert Smith— let's not be too formal, shall we? ("The Last Thing You Should Do"). This song sounds a bit familiar, oh, it can't be but it is. One of my very, very favorites — "Quicksand." What a lovely duet, what spectacular lyrics. My fact is wet — it's those old involuntary tears, but Kali is on cue with tissues in hand. This is the highlight of the evening for me. And that coat rack. A nice little side show watching David be assisted into his attire, primping and such. Love those frock coats!

Kali: I sure hope we get to sing Happy Birthday. Belle will be so disappointed if we don't. I wonder what he's singing now — I don't recognize it. As I turn to Belle to ask her, I notice that she's crying. She's actually *crying*! Is it her stomach?? Where'd I put those tissues?

Belle: ("Battle for Britain;" "Voyeur of Utter Destruction") This is pretty fascinating. We can't really see the cocoon, but we are looking straight on at David in the cut-out board. I must say, I always intrigued by the special effects. Kali will enjoy the video, as we haven't been able to really see the scrim screen. I can tell what's on it (as I've seen it before) but's it's been too loud for me to attempt to explain it to Kali.

Kali: What's with that big white thing? Cool, they're projecting his face on it. But why's he in that cutout? And when did he go in there? Did I blink? I must have been distracted by all those people walking around. Where are they going? Not to get drinks or food, they're coming back empty handed. Looking around, I even notice a guy behind me talking on the telephone. Go figure!

Belle: *Why* did I eat that pizza? The ripples in my stomach are starting to get larger. ("I'm Afraid of Americans;" "Looking for Satellites") I have to give David credit, a benefit party where everyone expects familiar tunes only to play the entire new album.

Kali: Why did she eat that pizza? Not as many oldies as I had expected, unless I'm not recognizing them. After all, I never even listened to this stuff until last September. Oh, wait. "I'm Afraid of Americans" – this is from the new album. I wonder why he's afraid of us?

Belle: The crowd is participating now. "Under Pressure" and "Heroes" have everyone back to life. The group around us was definitely waiting for Lou Reed, and I suppose I'm a bit curious. The Lou Reed album that has always stayed with me is *Berlin* although few seem to remember it. "Queen Bitch" is done very well. I remember a time in 1990 when David began this song, but stopped mid-way (I believe this may have been in St. Petersburg, FL) but this is really good now. "Waiting for The Man" seemed to be a given, didn't it? Here's a trivia question, didn't Tin Machine perform this at the end of their tour in 1991 or early 1992? ("Dirty Boulevard")

Kali: "Under Pressure!" I can sing along again. Oh my, he's singing "Heroes." I've liked this ever since Belle told me the story behind it — Berlin Wall and whatnot. So, that's Lou Reed. Why is everyone booing him? (Oh...it's Looooou [LOL]).

Belle: Watch David sing "Moonage Daydream" when he was in his 20s and see him at 50 and you just know things get better with age. Fabulous!

Kali: Oh, I LOVE this one! "Moonage Daydream!" I don't believe this — I've got chills! Oh, geez. Sigh...if Belle asks me one more time if we're gonna sing Happy Birthday....I wonder if I should start belting it out on my own in hopes of getting the whole place to join in. She'll be devastated if we don't sing!

Belle: Finally, we do get to sing Happy Birthday! And a cake! I haven't been to such a fun birthday party in ages! Wish we could do this every year!!!

Kali: Thank God!

Belle: I won't bore you with my thoughts of "All the Young Dudes;" suffice to say that it takes me back to a juke box in a bowling alley and I'm a mere 12 years old. I just love all of this! ("Jean Genie!") The audience is all on their feet. So am I, but my stomach has returned to ocean status and I'm contemplating using the bag the t-shirts are in for an alternate purpose. I can't leave now....oh...

Kali: This is fantastic! I jump to my feet along with everyone else. Wow, Belle is up, too! She must be feeling better!

Belle: I watching the singing of "Space Oddity" from behind the scrim. I am sure he is singing with his image, but I am most moved by the silence around the stage. No one is there, just David and his audience. Never one of my favorite songs, it comes off with an almost reverent tone and is a fitting close to a spectacular evening.

Kali: Oh, how wonderful. Bowie is all alone on stage with his guitar and fans. A wonderful finale. There's 19,000 of us, but this feels so intimate. We're each alone with him.

The Departure

Kali: I'm warm and dizzy with excitement. I really want to go
        to the hotel and party with the *Teenage Wildlife* group,
        but Belle is feeling really bad — and she's my ride home.
        There's a guy playing the flute. The Flintstones? Heh,
        wonder if Fred liked David Bowierock? In the lobby the
        posters are gone. The whole display is gone. Oh well, off
        to get some Roy Rogers chicken for the ride home.

Belle: I'm warm and dizzy and walking down a suspended
        escalator doesn't help matters. Once in the air, I feel a
        tad better, but I need to get on that train. Poor Kali, he
        really isn't ready to call it a night, but I'm just not up to
        any festivities. We exit the Garden to the sound of a flute
        playing the theme from the Flintstones...have a yabba,
        dabba do time...I think we did.

Disclaimer: The events described above are as our failing
memories recall them, and in no way should be considered the
actual sequence of events.

THE NIGHT DAVID
BOWIE SWORE AT ME!
Sam, USA

*T*HOUGH I'D SEEN AND loved Bowie's 1987 and 1995 tours, it was not until 1997 that my life and finances were in a place where I was able to take time off work and follow the tour around the States for a few weeks.

I didn't venture too far afield, only those tour dates closest to my home state of Virginia: Boston, Philadelphia, NYC, Washington and Atlanta. Not only did I want to experience how the set lists evolved night after night, but I had hopes of a meeting with Bowie himself and I spent days staking out hotels (which often turned out to be the wrong hotels) and wasting hours waiting outside stage doors while Bowie often rushed into the theater via a different entrance. For weeks and weeks, I had missed him. But failure only made me more determined to succeed, more fixated on exchanging a few words with the man.

My time following the tour was drawing to a close and my options were drying up. I was becoming more desperate. Since the venues on the 1997 tour were smaller club style theaters rather than stadiums, and since the tickets I had gotten were all general admission standing tickets, I figured there was no reason why

I couldn't try to jostle my way to the front of the stage and say something to Bowie in between songs. I guess I wanted to prove that I was a serious student of music who could connect with David on an intellectual level.

At the Capitol Ballroom in Washington, DC, I joined the line early but there were maybe a hundred people ahead of me already. By "Hallo Spaceboy" I had succeeded in pushing my way right to the front of the stage. I was absolutely focused on attracting Bowie's attention and in my head I rehearsed over and over what I planned to say to him. After "Little Wonder" he went to grab a bottle of water from the drum riser. As he drank from the bottle, I seized my big chance:

"Hi" I called.

Bowie looked right in my direction.

"Hi!" I yelled again. "What motivates your use of Neapolitan chords?"

"My use of *what*?" Bowie asked, looking right at me. "I didn't catch that."

"Neapolitan chords!" I shouted back.

"I haven't got a f★★★ing clue what you're talking about!" he laughed and signaled to drummer Zachary Alford to start the next song, just as someone behind me punched me in the shoulder and told me to "shut the f★★★ up and let the man sing."

A mere twenty seconds or so, but a connection nonetheless. How many other fans can say they've even had that? So David Bowie swore at me, but let me tell you something: the moment we made eye contact, every other person in the venue just melted away and those twenty seconds felt like an eternity. An eternity I will treasure for the rest of my life.

IF ONLY THERE WAS SOMETHING BETWEEN US...OTHER THAN OUR AVATARS

RaMoana, USA

*W*HEN WE FIRST JOINED *BowieNet*, we were given free membership and an installation CD of WorldsChat 3D Chat and BowieWorld was one of the Worlds. There was a Chaos Room to meet and dance in (to Bowie music, of course), and an Art Gallery with actual Bowie artwork on the walls to walk around and study (I remember "The Minotaur" and other *Outside*-ish art in there). It was a 3D interactive chat — you could text chat but also initiate a voice chat with other players — walk around other Worlds and, depending on what avatar you chose, you could even fly.

When you landed at the beginning of WorldsChat, you started as a penguin, but once in the Avatar Building you could walk around to pick your Avatar for your look. Sometimes I would be a pumpkin and plant myself on the ground next to the pathway at the Landing Site with just the top of the pumpkin sticking out so I could observe the comings and goings. People would walk around me and I was barely noticed. One time someone said, "Hey what are you doing?" I replied, "I'm ripening my pumpkin!"

I chose Pegasus as an avatar many times and you could fly and follow players into other Worlds or jump into mirrors and other dimensions as this flying white horse with huge wings. You could see the name of the player floating above their head. One time I decided to be cheeky and be a female avatar but with no clothes! I was just trying to see what reaction I would get. I was near the Landing Site milling around when I noticed an avatar all in black — stand up black collar and long flowing black cape and spikey hair! (Think Earthling Bowie, all in black but with no name floating above his head). There was no Avatar like that to select in the Avatar Building. I knew because I had studied them all.

It was none other than David Bowie himself — and I was naked! I walked up to him and said, "Well hello sailor, fancy meeting you here." He looked at me and said something like "You could do better." He was not impressed, turned and jumped to a BowieWorld gamma mark dimension. Little did he know, I knew how to follow. We landed in some corner on a hands building, but he quickly took off in some alley and I lost him. Needless to say, I spent lots of time after that going to WorldsChat hoping I would run into him again. I never did, but I always made sure I wasn't naked!

THE REUNION
Patti Brett, USA

⟨N September of 1995, a few of my friends and I went to see
David Bowie at Hershey Park on his Outside tour. After the
show, we bumped into Carlos Alomar who had been David's
rhythm guitarist and musical director on and off since 1974.
We had remained friends with Carlos since we met him during
the recording of *Young Americans* at Sigma Sound Studios in
Philadelphia.

Carlos was happy to see us and we, him. He mentioned the
band would be getting in to Philadelphia the day prior to their show
at the Blockbuster Center in Camden, New Jersey on September
22nd. Carlos thought it would be a great idea to have a reunion at
Doobies Bar, the bar I worked at in downtown Philadelphia. He
suggested we contact the old crowd and have a drink together.

We reached out to our friends and told them to meet us at
Doobies. Carlos contacted me and we set up a time. We all arrived
at the bar and had a wonderful time reminiscing, but several
people voiced their disappointment at not being able to talk to
David anymore.

Carlos told us that they were leaving directly from the show
the next night and were headed to Pittsburgh. He promised to
get us backstage passes for after the show and that David would

be there. Carlos put our friend Patrick in charge of making sure the passes got to everyone prior to the show and 20 passes were provided.

After the show, we all met at the backstage door. About 45 minutes went by and the backstage door opened with David standing there! He greeted each of us, giving us hugs and kisses and telling us it was great to see all of us. We walked down the hallway and into a large room where we chatted and caught up on what was happening with all of us. Some people had kids, some had not aged well, and some looked "exactly the same," David quipped, as he ran his fingers through his hair and told us *he* looked fabulous. I quickly grabbed the hair on his chin and said, "I don't know, I think you look a little grey there." We all had a laugh but one of my friends scolded me a bit for speaking to him that way. I really felt we had risen above the rock idol/fan stage and that I could speak to him as a person. "He's just a person," I reminded them.

We talked for hours and David's tour manager kept reminding him he need to get on the bus and they really needed to leave. David's response was very touching. He continued to tell the tour manager that he was talking to his friends and wasn't ready to leave yet. Finally, the tour manager said, "We have to leave now!" in a somewhat slightly agitated tone. "Not until we get pictures," cried David!! We took dozens of group photos and then he left.

About 10 days later, I was in Bristow, Virginia to see the show at the Nissan Pavilion. We had backstage passes again and when we went back, after the show, I noticed David had dyed that little patch of hair on his chin. It made my heart melt.

DON'T THANK ME, THANK DAVID

Sandra (Spidey) Atkins, UK

Astoria 1999

*W*ELL, IT ALL STARTED when we heard a hush hush story that DB "might" be performing a one off show in London! Whoo Hooo! We were so excited as DB himself was still saying in interviews that there would be no tour for another two years. A few days later, we found out that the show was going to happen and the name of the venue was the Astoria Theatre in London and it would be on 2 December 1999.

Right then —I'm on the case!

The first thing I did was book the train for us because if you book it enough in advance you get a good deal with the train fares. Then I had to ask my boss if I could "somehow" get a few hours off work the day of the gig, as I had *no* holiday left to take! My boss at the time was *wonderful* (the best boss in the world) and his exact words were "you have *got* to go, we'll sort something out about your hours, but you *are* going!"

I then got the phone number to the Astoria. I phoned them to see if I could get any more information. They denied all knowledge.

I didn't panic — it was early days yet. Then there was the "official" announcement of the gig on *BowieNet*, 100% confirmed. Ok, I thought, now I'll get some details so I rang the Astoria again. They still denied all knowledge. Next I phoned Virgin Head Offices in London and they said they had no information. I said I just wanted to know when tickets would go on sale and how they would go on sale. But they couldn't or wouldn't say.

I then phoned the Outside Organization with no luck. I managed to find out the event promoters were Solo Promotions, so I phoned them but with no luck. This went on for two solid weeks. I phoned the Astoria two times every morning and every afternoon. I phoned weekends too and checked the Net constantly for news.

Finally there was a breakthrough! The woman from the Astoria said, "Sorry I can't help you with information today love, but *do* keep trying." Whoo Hooo — you bet I will!

Eventually, I got some real information, but what they told me was that tickets would go on sale Monday, 22nd November for personal callers to the club only. Cash sales only! How were we supposed to get to London for 10 am on a Monday morning? My boss had already agreed to some time off and asking for more to go the Astoria to try and get a ticket was out of the question.

I was so distressed. I phone the Astoria to complain. I phoned the Outside Organization, Virgin Radio, Virgin Head Office, *BowieNet* — I nearly got hold of Richard Branson himself! But no luck for getting tickets.

The Outside Organization did say there would be other ways to get tickets, but they were very vague. Virgin Radio said "tune in next week for your chance to win a ticket." How was I supposed to listen to the radio every morning when I was at work? I wrote emails to *BowieNet* — to Howard, Ron Roy, to the info team — all with *no* responses! Then the news came that *some* tickets would be on sale on the Monday morning by phone! We're back in with a chance!

There were about six telephone numbers given out on the Net, plus I found another number that no one seemed to know anything about, and one of my friends gave me another "secret" number she had. These two special numbers were only given out to a handful of people, for real hardcore fans. So, as Monday morning drew closer, the anxiety and excitement grew and grew. A lot of people asked me to get them tickets, but I knew I needed to just stick with my purchase. If everyone got tickets for other people, those who did phone themselves would have less of a chance.

Monday morning came at last. My boss told everyone in the office to stop working — he gave them all the telephone numbers and instructions to start phoning just before 10 am. I had two numbers that hadn't been published — the Virgin one and Aloud. com and up until 9:44 am there was no trouble in getting through to these at all — but by 9:50 am they were constantly engaged. At 9:42 I had gotten through but was told to "ring back in 8 minutes" and the operator wouldn't let me hold.

At 10:02 one of my workmates shouted "I've got music on this line! I'm through!" I threw my phone across my desk and ran around to hers! Everybody in the office stopped what they were doing and ran round to cheer me — the girl on the other end of the phone said "Can I help you?" I somehow stuttered out the words, "Yes please. Two tickets for the David Bowie show at the Astoria." She said, "Hold on a minute please." I fumbled in my purse for my ever faithful credit card and waited. My boss meanwhile was jumping around the office shouting "She's got them!" Then the girl came back on the line and spoke those awful words:

"Sorry, they've all sold out."

I saw the whole office closing in on me. It was like looking down a tunnel. How the f★★★ did that happen? I couldn't talk. I went and sat back at my desk with everyone looking at me and not knowing quite what to say. I managed to thank everyone for trying and fought back the tears for just long enough to go and lock myself in the loo and have a good cry.

I phoned my friend Steph at work and was sad to hear it was the same story for her. Later in the afternoon, my nephew contacted me and said he could get away from work early and go to London to get tickets for us. I rang the Astoria, but they said tickets had sold out in 20 minutes. We were gutted. Absolutely devastated.

The Message Boards and Guest books exploded! Fans were not happy. But my friends kept saying "we'll get there…don't worry, we *have* to." Then *BowieNet* announced a ticket give-away. But, as I feared, it was only *one* ticket per person.

I didn't see a point in entering as there is no way on earth I would or could go without my husband Don. He's as big a fan as me and since 1978 we had been to every show together. But my friends said I must enter — that if we won one ticket then another one would be easy to sort out. And that I had to have faith. So I entered, not for a minute thinking I'd win.

On the Saturday of the draw, Steph phoned me and told me to "check my email" as the winners had been sent notification from Howard. Sure enough, I had won. But I couldn't get too excited. Don's face when I told him I'd won was a half-smile and also sad as I said "I am *not* going without you, Don."

I wrote to Howard at *BowieNet* again — a two page email — pouring my heart out and telling him it would break my heart to leave Don standing outside. I had a reply of four words: Sorry, no tickets left.

We tried everything: appeals on the boards, phone calls to all the organizations possibly involved and I offered to donate £100 to Children in Need if they could help us out, but nothing.

Friends kept saying it will all be sorted out, and we clung

to this hope. Tuesday night came — off to London for the *Jools Holland* TV show on which David was appearing. We found our friends and they all said they would ask around and try to get us a second ticket, but it seemed unlikely. I wished I had never entered the competition — it only seemed to make things more complicated.

I did want to make sure someone who deserved to go got my ticket and I thought of Gilly straight away. I knew she was going to take a chance and come to London from Germany. We tried to put on a brave face, but it did put a cloud over the evening.

We had a lovely time Tuesday night, the show was a fantastic experience, but all our other friends had tickets for Astoria and we felt a bit different and a bit lost. By the end of the evening, everyone was getting so excited for Astoria.

With only three hours sleep Tuesday night, we awoke on Wednesday very tired and very depressed. I went online again looking for some hope of how we could get in — still hoping for a miracle —but nothing. Don and I decided that we had nothing to lose by still going to London. We had bought and paid for the train tickets and I had done a lot of overtime to make up for my time off for work. We thought at the very worst we could see some friends, have a drink and I could find Gilly to tell her to say she was me and get in on the *BowieNet* Guest List.

I awoke with a start the day of the Astoria show. I quickly got ready for work, and then decided I'd take just one more look on the computer to see if anything had happened with tickets. I was surprised to see a couple of people online who I didn't usually see in the morning. Even Duncan (Bowie's son) was online. Strange — then I looked at the clock on the computer! I had gotten up 6 hours too early! I was really screwed up! Back to bed.

Don picked me up from work that day at 2:00 pm and we went home to get ready. We hadn't even thought about what we would wear. Steph phoned me. She was in London with a few of the others that were going. I told her we were coming down just to see people and have a drink and if by some miracle we got in, then that would be a bonus. We got into London at 5:30 pm and made our way slowly to the Astoria.

Don said we'd find out what the touts [scalpers] were asking, but we didn't hold out much hope. The cheapest tickets we'd found was £100. One of our friends had paid £250! We got to the club to find hundreds of touts! I knew this would be the case — I knew the touts had gotten most of the tickets. They kept coming up to us and we asked how much, but they were saying £90 or £80.

Then this guy came to us and we told him we wanted two tickets so we couldn't pay a fortune. He said he'd let us have two at £60 each. We haggled a bit, said we only had £100 and then settled on £110 for the two tickets.

We were really pleased. Plus we would be in the club together and I could give my place on the guest list to Gilly once we found her. I thought we could settle down and go get a drink with friends when Don said "we should check that these tickets are genuine." I had never given it a thought!

We went into a bookshop where there was light and got the tickets out. You only had to take one look at them in good light to know they were fakes. We'd been ripped off. We were devastated. We knew lots of people standing in line outside the club so we found someone and asked to see his ticket. Sure enough, it was different — our tickets even had the same number on them — 000170. The owner of the real tickets looked at ours and said "you've been had."

We went off trying to find the guy who sold them to us, not thinking we really would, but Don thought it was still early and the guy probably wouldn't have wanted to go home yet. Low and behold, we found the little weasel! We went to confront him. We didn't have an aggressive attitude: I just said I wasn't comfortable with the tickets. He said that was fine and he gave us our money back. Then I wondered if maybe they were real. But Don doubted it and said the guy didn't want any trouble early in the night.

We found more friends standing in line and was telling them about our narrow escape when the guy standing behind our friends said "did you buy them off a guy wearing a Russian hat?" We said "yeah, that's the guy." He got his ticket out and sure enough—— number 000170. He ran off to find the guy and to tell security now that we were sure they were fake.

Within minutes the place was crawling with police and security guards. They were going up and down the line checking tickets with ultra violet pens. The touts ran off in all directions. We knew then we wouldn't be able to buy a real ticket from a tout.

We found Steph and Paul and the others in a pub and told them the story of our fake tickets. Steph said to come to the Astoria with them as they were about to leave. We didn't feel like it, but we went anyway. Steph still insisted we would get in and that we had to have faith.

It was very hard. We stood on the opposite side of the barriers, watching our friends go in the Guest List entrance where I knew my name was written down. I hugged Steph as she went thought the doors, and fought back the tears. I wished them all a great time, then we walked away.

We asked around if anyone had seen Gilly. I needed to make sure she got in. Someone said she had been seen around the back of the club, by the stage entrance. We went around back and there were about eight or nine people standing there, including Gilly. She had just arrived in London and still had her flight bag with her. The guy who we met who also had a fake ticket was there also as were two others that had the same problem. They were asking to talk to the tour manager who came out and spoke with them. A few minutes later, the Tour Manager came with passes to let those three in and also let in a guy who had a ticket for Gisborne with him. We thought that was a nice gesture.

I called the Tour Manager over and told him our story. How I already was on the guest list, but how I wouldn't go in without Don and that we had bought the fake tickets and it was us who alerted people and stopped other fans from being ripped off. He said he sympathized, but couldn't help. There were no more tickets or passes. He did say he could get us into the Milan or Copenhagen shows, but we knew we couldn't go to either of them. We were gutted and I had tears in my eyes. I told him we understood and "by the way, my name is Sandra Atkins, Spidey." He again said he was sorry and went back inside.

The doors were still open and two security guys stood there. We could see lots of people going past inside the door, something was going on! Then Gilly spotted Eric (Bowie's bodyguard) and shouted to him "Eric, please help us." Eric looked out at us all and then went away.

A couple of minutes later Eric came back outside. He called Gilly over and motioned to me and Don too. He said to Gilly, "who are you with tonight?" Gilly pointed to me and Don and said "Don and Sandra Atkins." Eric said, "I know about them. You three, follow me — I have no tickets, but *David Wants You Three Inside!*"

We were in a daze. Was this really happening? We were walking up this corridor with Eric and I kept saying "Thank you Eric." He turned around and said, "Don't thank me, thank David. He saw you and he wants you in." OMG —– can you believe it? Gilly and I kept hugging each other and Don and I were thanking her too. Gilly the miracle worker — and to think we had gone to find her to make sure that she would get inside.

We went through the entrance at the top of some stairs and we were *right in front of the bloody stage*! *WhoooHooooo*!

The three of us were grinning like Cheshire cats. We had time to go to the bar which was still empty (most of the fans were still standing in line outside the club). We asked Gilly, the expert, where the best place to stand would be and she said "follow me." Boy, were we happy to do that. We had a fantastic view — right at the front of the stage.

Soon the people outside were let in and started to crowd around us. Everyone was grinning and hugging each other. All of the emotion of the previous few weeks came to a head. When David walked on stage he looked right over to where Don, Gilly and I were and he waved at us! *I went wild*!! I have never "let go" so much at a gig. I just could not believe it wasn't all a dream.

The show was fantastic. David was really enjoying it, even though he was still full of a cold. It was one of the best nights of our lives, one to remember for always.

Miracles do happen — Steph was right.

Thank you David, Thank you Eric, Thank you Gilly

Postscript 1999

A lot of people have asked "how" we got in, but I decided not to shout about our story. There were a lot of real fans who didn't get in that night and a lot of them who were ripped off by fake tickets too. They must have felt bad enough without hearing about how fortunate we were — we thought it was best to keep it quiet and just say we got lucky.

Postscript 2016

In 2016 I feel I can tell our story to anyone who will listen. "A real life adventure, worth more than pieces of gold" indeed.

I GOTTA MESSAGE FOR
THE ACTION MAN
RaMoana, USA

$\mathscr{I}$T ALL STARTED A month before NetAid (1999) when AMan (aka my husband, David) said to me, after a visit to the Bnet Chatroom and hearing the NetAid excitement, "you know, I quite fancy a trout fishing holiday in the UK." AMan knew I was a bit down about the no Bowie tour announcement and two years since our fabulous Bowie fix in Ft. Lauderdale. A trip to the UK, using one ticket with hard earned frequent flyer miles and staying with my best mate, Annette, made it a feasible idea. I set to work planning and getting NetAid tickets (not easy to do from across the pond), before AMan could change his mind. It was also our 10th wedding anniversary and a birthday present to me. 10 years ago to the day, I had arrived in the UK and a month later, AMan and I married in the small borough of High Wycombe....that's another story.

In the meantime, rumors abounded about the *TFI Friday* show and a Bowie appearance the night before NetAid. We were of the feeling, just get to the UK, perhaps a small gig would be in the works by the time we arrived. Anxiety descending and excitement was building, the closer we got to our October 1st departure date.

Many personal and business situations were also coming to a head, so it was all a bit of chaos before we left.

I managed to call the UK for *TFI* tickets at some ungodly hour and mumbled into the phone about being the only Yanks to come across the pond for NetAid and would love to see Bowie on the 8th at *TFI*. The chap replied, "Well you are coming from Florida, so I'll just have to let you in, now won't I?" And my name was added to the guest list, with two guests. This woke me up and got me into gear - we were going to see Bowie! At least twice!

I quickly sent a message to David Bowie (via Ask David on BNet) because I heard he does read the submissions, albeit answers very few. So, not expecting a reply, but wanting my situation known, I sent a message to the real Action Man that basically said, "I don't take kindly to the English weather, but I'm making the journey to see you. Please make it HOT ("If I'm Dreaming My Life" would do it for me)."

Side note: right after I sent the message, the phone rang and I thought "oh gawd! He's ringing me up!" — it was Annette, finalizing arrangements.

We got to the UK a week before the Bowie events — I got a quick fix of finding some Bowie in the Virgin Store at Gatwick upon arrival, procuring a couple of the singles, "Thursday's Child." I manage to go to HMV in Aylesbury during the week and find *Hunky Dory* and *Scary Monsters* on CDs — no promo *Hours* material at this store, however.

Friday finally comes — it's October the 8th, exactly two years since I met Bowie in Fort Lauderdale and got the 3+ hour's concert — we set out on our rail and tube journey to Hammersmith for the *TFI* taping. Two hours later we are there. We finally locate the studios and I am practically in Steph's face before realizing, it's her! At long last I find Steph and Carl! I receive hugs all around and I think: finally the Bowie family is all together, but where is Paul? I get into queue, order A Man to get us drinks, and promptly we are told we can only drink on the other side of the street. I felt I was back in England for sure now. The glamorous Helen arrives and I finally feel calm and all is right with the world. So doors open, we check our gladrags (coats) and handbags, then proceed to the bar until the studio doors open. I chat up the security man, as you do, at one of the side doors and glean the info I need about which are doors for what. We don't want upstairs for the interview, we want downstairs for the best stage jockeying position. We are finally corralled to one of three stages and I am up front for the Eurythmics, by the small steps that the performers use to get on and off the stage. A riveting performance was given by Annie Lennox. I tell the cool backup singers, upon their descent off the stage, about how beautifully they sang and thanked them and they are grateful for the comment! We are then supposed to move position to the next stage for a performance by the Charlatans — not wanting to lose my fab position on this stage, I hang back and stand between the two stages, ready to run back if need be. Chris Evans, the show host, appears and I notice a camera aimed at me in his line of fire. I find the nearest security and tell them we need to get near the stage for Bowie and I am told which stage Bowie will be at (same stage as Eurythmics). I sidle back to that side, and by now knowing the deal, I begin directing audience members like the camera crews do, making way for various wires and cameras, moving people about and back to their shuffled position. We watch the Bowie interview on the monitors, though it was hard for me to concentrate on the interview.

Gail Ann Dorsey breezed past me and as I turned around, I was face to face with her, I was so taken by surprise to even see her, I said "*Ohhh Hello Gail!*" and she turned and said hello back to me with a beautiful smile and a direct look. I got chills just from the sight of her. It was then the excitement started to get to me and Bowie appeared and descended the steep steps to the floor and right past me and I manage to touch his shoulder with

a "hallo sailor". I felt like I was in the chatroom again, as he gave
no response. Ha! Don't you know, you were touched by the hand
of Moaner (again!), sailor boy!?

I can't even recall what Bowie word was spoken but the songs
performed transformed me to that special place Bowie always
knows how to take me — you know the one, like you and him
are the only one left in the world and it ain't such a bad place
then, is it? He started with "Survive," followed by "China Girl"
and "Rebel Rebel." I love this version of "Rebel Rebel" by the
way — the only Reevesless rendition I accept (sorry but those
two other guitarists don't add up to Reeves!). I try to catch Mike
Garson's eye, as I know he would recognize me if he saw me, but
to no avail. Bowie seems to want to perform more but it all ends
abruptly and the cameras are off — Bowie leaves the stage and
goes past me again, this time surrounded by security, though I
still manage another grab on his shoulder (the right one this time),
but he leaves.

It's all over so we go back to the bar and hang out a bit, taking
pictures of our newly gained Bowie tie amongst ourselves and
rumors are that he may even walk through the section we are in
on his way out. We reluctantly go outside to breathe the Bowieless
air and hear more rumours that he is doing another interview
across the road and may catch him leaving there. That doesn't pan
out and a few of us make our way to the Edwards pub. We get
some much needed food and wait for the Bowie fans to arrive.
Steph and Spaceface have set up a fabulous room above the pub
and we are well treated with food and Bowiefare. I lend my new
Hours CD to the cause before the arrivals. Soon the mayhem
begins and I finally meet Ian, Adi, Zardoz and others. I gain
more Bowie insight from Paul and "why doesn't Bnet give some
promotional material to the cause" is my feeling, as the room is
also filled with UK fans that are want to join *BowieNet*, some have
tried for months, to no avail!

More drink and I try to ensure everyone knows where to meet for NetAid. I notice a table of Italians and make my way there to find they already know me! And Stefano and Paola greet me like a long lost relative. Pictures are taken throughout and the evening ends, with us having to leave as the party gets rolling! Having to take the train back to Aylesbury, 11 pm leaving time is our best bet.

NetAid 9th Oct — quick meet up at the Greyhound pub and a bite to eat and more drink. We all had the mother of all queues to get into NetAid, each with varying entrances. The amount of people is astounding and my first ever concert this size. It's a bit daunting but as long as I drink, I'm okay. We manage to meet up again once inside, which is amazing in itself. And I spot Steph and company in some seats on the right front part of the stadium, and we rest our weary bones into some seats. The stadium is not filled to capacity but most of the crowd is on the pitch. The ones seated fight boredom and start numerous waves that reverberate around the stadium. Annette and I even did a 2-man wave in our hungover state — "eh", *pause* reply "eh" — that was it! Eventually even that small wave did its reverberation and the other side of the stadium eventually *waved* big time! The evening gets colder and even the blow up aliens don their jumpers.

After hours of waiting for the man, I know the moment arrives when Angelica Houston says something about "the legendary, the one and only..." and Bowie ambles on stage and says something about "it's lonely up here, glad you're out there" and starts singing "Life on Mars". That transfixed, glazed look overcomes me once again. I am standing on a seat and taking pics, trying to capture the moments. Steph and Spaceface had brought their "Hello Sailor" sign down in the crowd and Bowie receives their message, and notedly changes the lyrics to "look at those *sailors* go!" More songs (a total of 6), during "Pretty Things Are Going to Hell," I notice I am the only one around me singing it loudly and proudly, by now I had committed the words to heart (having had a copy of *Hours* two weeks prior to the release date! Ha!). Before I know it, I'm grooving on "Rebel Rebel" again and it's ended!

We make our way outside Wembley and get a few snaps outside. I end the roll when me and Steph find a wall right outside Wembley Stadium, covered in *Hours* posters, a befitting end, the hours are up!

I didn't get, "If I'm Dreaming My Life" (not performed until Vienna) and we didn't get any special benefits from Bowie (aside from the lyric change) or *BowieNet* for being *BowieNet* members — but we did get each other and that means the most. Seeing the excitement of Steph, Spaceface, Carl, Gilly, Spidey, Bianca, Simone, Adi, Ian, Paul, Stevek, Annette, Helen and others made the trip for me. To Spaceface and Steph I say a big *thanks* for making it a truly special event and organizing a slap up party. Oh yes, and the skillful AMan managed 10 rainbow trout in one day. Well-fed and somewhat Bowie-sated (is it ever enough!?), we made our return.

RAINING LIKE CRAZY — NYC 2006

Simone Metge, Germany

On November 2006, I flew to New York to attend the Black Ball concert at Hammerstein Ballroom. Coincidentally I was staying in a hostel that was rather close to the venue, so a day before the show I went to the venue in hopes of seeing David at the sound check. This was really weird actually, as they always seemed to do the sound check on the day of the show.

It was raining like crazy the whole day. Next to the back entrance was a construction site where I could stand underneath a roof, but I got soaked anyway. My umbrella wasn't of any use either. After a few hours I thought it was pointless to keep waiting, and left. I went to the Apple Store to check my emails, but I was restless and didn't really want to walk around at all, so I went back to the venue. I had planned on going to the cinema to watch *Prestige*, but since the venue was on the way to my hostel where I had to change my clothes, I decided to have one more look at the backstage door.

Suddenly I saw Nick Belshaw, David's stage manager. I don't think he knew or recognized me, but I asked him if David was there and he said "no, not yet" or something like that. I don't quite remember exactly what he said, but I knew then he really was going to come or that maybe he was already inside.

I kept on waiting in the rain and at some point a car pulled up and David got out and rushed inside the building, well hidden by a few security people who were in front of the backstage door. It all happened so fast that I couldn't do anything and security blocked my view.

So while David was inside, I chatted with one security guy, trying to convince him to not block my view when David came back out. I told him that I've met David several times before and that he knows me. The security guy didn't believe me. Security also tried to convince me to leave, as it would take a long time before he'd come out again…blah…blah…yeahhhh…right! I didn't move one bit!

Indeed it didn't take very long at all until the door opened again and I saw David coming. The security guys started to block my view again, but right at the second the door opened I yelled "*David!!!*"

Fortunately he heard me! "Hi, how are you my love" he asked and within a second we were standing in front of each other. Four security guys got in front of me right away, but David said "no no, it's ok!" so they left me alone.

We greeted each other with a kiss in each corner of the mouth. Right afterwards he jumped into the waiting car, saying he had to go because it was cold.

Yeah, tell me about that! I was dripping from rain, looking like a wet cat. I only managed to ask the first thing that came to my mind — if he had seen Placebo the night before — which he said he didn't. And then he was off.

Even though it was a very short time with David, it was just so sweet and I was running down the street in a daze, and then had to come back as I actually managed to forget my umbrella.

The security guy was still there and completely stunned that I told him the truth before.

The next day when I returned with other fans that same security guy handed me a program as a present. I didn't actually tell anyone about my encounter the day before as I wanted it to be my sweet little secret.

I was so glad I saw him the day before, because when he arrived for the actual show in the evening he rushed in right away, and only signed very few things for some other people in haste.

That night Bowie performed his three last songs ever on stage: "Wild Is The Wind", "Fantastic Voyage" and "Changes" as a duet with host Alicia Keys.

THE WORLD IS DIFFERENT NOW (AND WE ARE ALL CHANGED)

BOWIE: ROCK OF AGES
Will Putney, USA

$\mathcal{T}$ODAY WAS A VERY strange day to say the least. It almost feels kind of wrong to be this upset today. It feels sort of shameful and kind of self-indulgent to mourn a rock star, someone you had never met in person, in the same way and with the same depth you would mourn the loss of a friend or family member. These lines seem very blurry to me today, as David Bowie was an honorary member of one side of my family, thanks to my Uncle Frank. I grew up listening to Bowie from the time I was in the cradle. Over the 40 years that I have been alive, he was an omnipresent force that consciously and sub-consciously guided and shaped me in so many ways. The albums Uncle Frank loaned to me and the mix tapes he made for me in the 80s were as precious as spun gold to the pre-teen and teenage me. All of my fondest memories of holidays, birthdays and other family gatherings have Bowie soundtracks laced into them. I essentially became the rabid fan of music that I am today due in large part to my Uncle Frank and his fandom of David Bowie, which he very gracefully passed down to me over the past four decades.

I was fortunate enough to see Bowie live over 30 times, with my first show being the 1987 Glass Spider Tour at Veterans Stadium in Philadelphia. I was 12 years old. Bowie shows were more than just concerts to me, they were family events. Those nights contain some of the most precious memories that I hold on to today. It pained me deeply when it became apparent that Bowie was no longer going to tour; not only because of the fact that the world would be forever void of the pure awesomeness that was a Bowie show, but it also took away another chance to spend time with my uncle which is an increasingly rare treat. Now, with David Bowie's death, the concept of our very limited time on this earth and that fact that no one here gets out alive has more gravity than ever.

Although David Robert Jones was always just a mere mortal man, with flesh and blood that flowed like yours or mine, his Bowie persona projected a sense of immortality, a notion of otherworldliness and transcendence above all norms. While thoughts about what the day that Bowie passed on would be like did cross my mind occasionally, I naively wanted to believe that the man who sold me my world would live on forever. Fortunately, for all of us, his art, music and amazingly impactful legacy as David Bowie will do just that.

Rest in peace David and thank you for everything.

RAINBOWS IN JANUARY
Jennifer Staib, USA

$\mathcal{O}$F MY LIFE WERE to be mapped out or made into some tangible shape, it would take the form of David Bowie's silhouette or perhaps even a lightning bolt. I cannot remember much of my life when Bowie wasn't breathing into my soul. It is not an exaggeration to say that the person I am today has been shaped by him.

I grew up in the 1980s in Philadelphia and my brother was a musician so our home was constantly filled with music. In the summer of 1986, I was seven years old when my family packed into the big white Oldsmobile station wagon and headed to the theater in Feasterville. We were going to see *Labyrinth*. I can remember standing in the lobby and studying the movie poster. I was captivated by the image of this person with long, spikey blonde hair and cool makeup. I still remember that moment when the Goblin King appeared on screen. His voice held me. Something about him left me completely mesmerized.

As my dad drove us home, I grilled my family on this David Bowie person. He was all I could think about. In the following weeks I was given singles from *Labyrinth* and a copy of the *Never Let Me Down* album. I scanned MTV for videos. At that time, they would typically play "Let's Dance", "Modern Love" or "Day In, Day Out" a few times a day. How I wished I could have gone to the 1987 Glass Spider show. A special on TV called "Backstage Bash with Bowie" featuring videos and an interview with Bowie was shown on TV. We also had a recording of the concert that I would play over and over again. This was my first introduction to Bowie's live performances and I was smitten.

My childhood wasn't easy. While I had a good family life, I didn't have a good time in school or with my peers. I was a social outcast and bullied or tormented almost on a daily basis. I wanted to belong so badly. I was desperate for friends. But the constant stream of hate made me more shy and withdrawn. As I transferred to a new school, being a David Bowie fan made me more of a target. A Catholic School, our creative writing class let us cover our books in pictures or artwork of our choice. I covered my books in photos of Bowie — many from the Ziggy Stardust era. Somehow this translated into Bowie was a sinner and I was going to hell for being a fan. But out of this came my activism for the LGBTQ community for which I have become a strong advocate.

Somewhere in all of this turmoil I learned something from David Bowie. I learned that there was no comfort or grace in conforming. I learned that putting my true self aside to make others more comfortable with me would only bring me misery. Bowie taught me to be myself.

I went to my first concert in 1990. It was the Sound and Vision Tour and my dad took me. I was 12 years old. Bowie spoke through a lot of his songs and relayed humorous stories from Philadelphia visits of his past. I distinctly remember him talking about a group of people in the front of the audience, telling us they had been following him since the 1970s. I now know he was talking about the infamous Sigma Kids who attended the recording of *Young Americans* in Philadelphia.

The advent of the internet brought me more Bowie immersion than I ever thought possible. I had once felt so alone as a Bowie fan, but then discovered websites like *Teenage Wildlife* and *BowieNet* where there were so many more people just like me. I met a girl who would later officiate at my wedding, and I met Patti — one of the Sigma Kids.

Bowie's songs always played in the background of events both significant and ordinary in my life. Somehow, the universe would always find a way to throw his music to me at a difficult time when I would need to hear that voice and be reminded of what strength looked like. My first born child bears David Bowie's name. The little girl who was so star struck in her post *Labyrinth* haze back in the 80s declared she would name her first son after Bowie. And I did. I wanted my child to be inspired by a person who knew it was more than ok to express yourself and to be who you wanted to be. Someone who didn't feel the need to be a follower.

This year has been rough. On January 10, 2016, I was out with my children. We had an odd warm day and a thunderstorm. A rainbow appeared in the sky and we hopped out of the car to admire it and take a photo. Rainbows in January are so incredibly rare in Pennsylvania and I remember telling my kids it was special. I told them that something special was happening somewhere. Indeed it was. The next day, at 5:30 am, the maintenance man at my job came to my desk and told me that David Bowie had died. I laughed at him because…duh, Bowie is immortal, right? My shaky hands typed "David Bowie" into Google and the worst news was true. I finished my shift even though my mind was spinning and my heart was desperate to let the tears flow. The whole world felt different. I did what my instincts tell me to do when I experience great loss — I went to a tattoo parlor and had Bowie's name permanently placed into my forearm. A few months later I added his face.

After 30 years I still have found ways to be inspired by Bowie. I suspect I will never cease to be amazed.

MOON BLUE
Theresa Bradley, UK

   HAVE THREE STORIES TO share, but cannot decide which one to choose as I have many, many wonderful memories regarding David Bowie. Shall it be the first time I attended his concert at the Liverpool Empire in 1973? Or perhaps in 1976, bunking off school and missing a maths exam to be in London at the Wembley Empire Pool on the mind-blowing Isolar Station to Station tour? Another treasured moment in time was following the Stage tour around the country in the summer of 1978, but that would be an entire book in itself! Back then, tickets would arrive through the post in a self-addressed envelope and when you opened that envelope to find your ticket for the show and hold it in your hand, pure delight! Or queueing outside a theatre and securing a ticket after a long wait. However, I have opted for another story to share with you.

It's Sunday evening, back home from work at 6:30 pm. Having recently updated to a smart phone, I was having a great time watching and searching for the many fantastic Bowie items available. Later on that night, I was viewing the Liverpool comedian Alexie Sayle singing "Hello John, gotta new motor?" Laughing at the lyrics, then watching him performing "Dr. Martens Boots" on the *Young Ones* hilarious TV series. I go to bed with this song in my head and it's still making me smile.

Monday and there goes the alarm, pause it a short while, then I'm out of bed making myself a nice cup of tea. I find myself stomping my feet and singing the chorus to "Dr. Martens Boots" and it's still continuing to make me smile. I place my small portable radio on the shelf in the hallway. My flat is all on the same level so this enables me to hear it whichever room I'm in. The heating is slowly but surely coming on and my sweet tea tastes really good. Not too bad for a Monday morning.

Was that David Bowie's name mentioned? The words and sounds are confusing to me, it must be another David someone. Go to the bedroom and check my phone, no news there, and then I hear those words properly, clearly, starkly for the first time…

Never watch TV in the daytime but on it goes. Images of Bowie everywhere and my phone is now flashing like crazy. Dead. Time stands still.

I start shaking from head to toe. The news reporters continue to mispronounce his name and I swear out loud at the TV screen. It's Bowie as in rainbow, not the bough of a tree! I shake more with anger. Can't seem to move, I'm in shock and my limbs feel so heavy yet also weightless.

I continue to stare and stare at the television, transfixed. I call my Mum and sister Chris to tell them and they too are shocked. "Just letting you know, but I'm OK and chat with you later." Funny how we use the term OK when we are very, very far from OK.

I message Lucy my Bowie freak friend up in Scotland as my phone goes into meltdown. I decide to leave other calls till much later as I have heard from those I needed to speak with on this life changing morning.

The days and nights that followed seemed so surreal. As for the tributes that quickly followed — very few were wonderful. Most I found to be an insult to his memory.

A few days after the announcement of his passing, I went into Liverpool city centre and his image and music seemed to be everywhere. Something catches my attention in the shop window, moon blue, soft leather Doc Martens. I always loved the zig-zagged laced up boxing boots Bowie wore early on in his career — even had a pair myself in the seventies — but I can't really afford the £105 price tag so soon after the Christmas holidays. The boots just scream Bowie at me, so I try a pair on and treat myself. Comfort shopping? Retail therapy? Whatever. I refer to them as my Bowie Docs. Perhaps I was feeling a slight sense of guilt by the fact I had been laughing at the song when the tragic news broke that morning.

2016 has been so cruel in many ways, each month bringing new sorrows. It has to be the worse year of my life and I have had fifty seven of them.

In my photo you can see the Bowie Docs, my Bowie cushion which I purchased when he was still alive and a chair which reminds me of one of the photo shoots from the Ziggy Stardust era. This chair belonged to my beloved Mother Emily, who joined David in the moon blue sky on August 23 of this cruel, wicked year.

Love and peace to you all.

WHY DAVID BOWIE IS IMPORTANT TO ME
Patti Brett, USA

As a fan of David's since 1972, when I was 17 years old, he taught me that it was ok to be different. He also taught me that not only was it ok to be different, it was ok to not care what people thought about me. I have carried that message with me my entire life.

David Bowie taught me so much more as well. Music, art, literature and travel all became important in my life. He expanded my mind and inspired me to not be afraid to try new and adventurous things. He was my enabler as he taught me to listen to things, looks at things, read things, go places and do things that were all out of my comfort zone.

Through his music, David provided me with the soundtrack to my life. I can tell you what was going on by looking back on what album was current or if he was touring. His music has brought me great joy, even when I thought I was as low as I could go. David always brought me back to a happier place.

Then, there was the sheer joy of seeing David perform live. Always funny, always emotional, he interacted well with his audiences and gave us memorable performances. He was gracious and sincere to his fans, both on and off stage, and very rarely cancelled a show so as not to disappoint us. David certainly never let us down.

David gave so much of himself, yet managed to have a private life, for which I admire him. I cannot imagine how difficult that must be to always be in the public eye — and yet we often had no idea what he was up to.

I will never forget David. He was such a huge part of my life. It's been said that David Bowie is a part of the fabric of the universe and I would have to agree. He is what grounds me.

CHANGING THE WORLD
Sandra (Spidey) Atkins, UK

$\mathcal{O}$ WAS ON THE BUS into work on Monday morning when I heard the news. I had been chatting to a neighbor when another lady came and sat near us. She asked if I'd heard the terrible news, and I immediately thought the university had blown up or something. When she said that David Bowie had died, I went into shock. I very nearly swore at her. What was she talking about, stupid woman…but I could see by her face she was telling the truth. I didn't know where to turn. The lady next to me tried to pick back up on our chittle chattle and I wanted to scream at her to *shut up*! I got off the bus as soon as I got into town, my hands shaking as I phoned my husband Don at work. Bless him — he had heard the news on the car radio. He was having a lift into work from a colleague so he couldn't turn the car around to go back home. I wish we had been together when we heard the news. Getting through work on Monday was nearly impossible. I was a wreck and just wanted to get home and be with Don. When we saw each other that evening, I just fell into his arms and we both sobbed our hearts out.

If you know Don and I, then you know what a huge part of our lives Bowie is. Our first ever conversation when we met in January 1978 was about Bowie. Don said he'd seem him in concert in 1976 and asked me if I'd like to go and see him in the summer, during his next tour. I was thrilled that Don already had plans to be seeing me in six months' time! He later told me he would have had no problem finding a home for his other ticket!

So there we were, Bingley Hall, Stafford, Summer of 1978 and my life was changed forever. I remember my knees giving way when Bowie came on stage and the force of the crowd as they all surged forward. I think I might have been squished if I'd fallen to the floor, but Don's friend Ray saw what was happening and helped me keep on my feet. I think Don was too engrossed himself to have noticed.

We saw Bowie many times over the next thirty plus years. We were so lucky, even managing to attend some really intimate gigs and TV performances. Such precious memories. Oh, for a time machine.

We also met so many good friends through *BowieNet*, *Bowie WonderWorld* and *Teenage Wildlife*. These are friends we will have forever, and we are so thankful, especially now, to be able to communicate with people who really "get it." As much as family and "other friends" try and understand, it's not the same. That's not their fault, they just can't.

We have also been incredibly lucky and managed to meet David a few times, albeit briefly snatched "hello's and thank you's" as we were getting things signed after a gig. And, of course, there was the HMV signing where we got to have a few more precious seconds with him. I remember my hands were trembling when I approached David, and he was such a gentleman and tried to put me at east. For years, I had wondered what I might say when or if I ever got the opportunity, but all I actually managed to blurt out was "I'm terrified" and David laughed and smiled that crooked smile, twinkle in his eye, put his hands on top of my trembling ones and said "are ya…"

Bowie's music is so diverse and there is an album for every mood.

It is impossible to pick a favorite, it changes depending on one's mood or state of life! But it's always been there, always a constant, always a help at the most difficult times. The hospital even played Bowie to Don while he was having Proton Beam Radiotherapy treatment for his eye cancer. Don strapped into an execution chair, but Bowie calmed him and eased the process for him. Back at the hotel after one of our scarier hospital appointments, "Wild is the Wind" was playing through the PA system. We looked at each other and smiled and knew that meant it would be OK.

After Bowie had "retired" following his heart problems, we didn't expect that we would see him in concert again, but we always kept a glimmer of hope — maybe some TV stuff or such? But it wasn't to be. We could expect no more, he had already given us so much (even "gifting" us Arcade Fire, who we discovered early on in 2005 only because of David. We have had the magic of their early gigs and a whole world more of special friends — some not surprisingly crossing over from the Bowie world).

Don and I have been de-cluttering over the past few years, preparing for our next chapter in life and the move to our forever home in Devon. Yet we have not been able to part with any of our Bowie memorabilia — magazines, videos, books, ticket stubs, badges (I still wear a Bowie badge every day and at 54 years old I don't ever intend to stop!). We used to buy every magazine and newspaper that had a Bowie feature, often buying two (one to keep pristine, one to read). On Tuesday, 12 January 2016, on my bus into work I picked up the *Metro*. The whole front page was Bowie's picture. I went to pick up a second copy out of habit, but put that one back. With this story, one is more than enough. I still haven't looked at it. I got home that night and pulled out one of our many Bowie "storage boxes" and just put the newspaper on top — my heart breaking again.

That David is no longer on this planet is surreal. From the euphoria of the new album arriving on Friday to the bombshell news a few days later. Six months on and I am still struggling so much to process this. This is *not* how it was supposed to be — he was always going to outlive us. How can he leave us like this and what the hell are we supposed to do now? I keep trying to tell myself that nothing has changed in our daily lives, it's not like we were in contact with him. In fact, up until *The Next Day* appeared out of nowhere in 2013, we had been through years of not expecting any new music or appearances. But still, there was always the hope, always the possibility and he was always out *there* — our guide, our mentor, our inspiration, our hope, our memories, our passion, our magic, our love...

The world is different now.

THE RELIC

Patrick Bamburak, USA

$\mathcal{O}$N 2006, THE COSTUME Institute of the Metropolitan Museum of Art in New York mounted an exhibition called "Anglomania: Tradition and Transgression in British Fashion."

The exhibition focused on the period from 1976 through 2006 and included designs by punk patrons Malcom McLaren and Vivienne Westwood, couture by *les incroyable* John Galliano, headwear by milliner Phillip Treacy, and of specific interest to me, the instantly iconic Union Jack frock coat commissioned by David Bowie and designed by London's *enfant terrible* Alexander McQueen.

The cover of Bowie's 1996 album *Earthling* depicted him wearing the coat, standing with his back to the camera, his hands clasped and his frame impossibly thin. He stood in a wide stance that seemed to lengthen the white fimbriations that framed the Union Jack's red and blue ordinaries.

The coat was stained and striped with razor cuts that gave the impression of slashes and injury.

With his face away from the camera, there was no way to discern Bowie's facial expression. Did he wear the stoic face that one would find on a member of The Queen's Guard? The silhouette of the coat gave the impression of a military uniform, but it was also distressed. Its condition implied the faded glory of the Empire.

With a ticket in hand, I went to the Met to see the exhibition. The crowd of museum goers was thick. I worked my way through the galleries until I turned a blind corner and finally saw the coat draped over a mannequin behind a thick glass pane.

As if I was before the man himself, I stepped forward and straightened my spine. I tried to get a sense of our comparative sizes. We may have been the same height, or perhaps I was slightly taller.

But my arms would never fit into those sleeves, nor could the coat stretch over the width of my shoulders.

It looked well-worn. The coat had the glossy patina of an old tapestry. It seemed to have a weight to it, the fabric heavy and durable despite its condition.

It must have been uncomfortably hot to wear under the stage lights.

This was not the casual stage-wear of a grunge rocker of the era. It was the tailored and tattered uniform of a prince.

Bowie was alive on that particular day of the exhibition, as I stood before the coat.

Now he is no longer living and my memory of the coat has assumed the form that a memory has when one thinks of the time they saw a holy relic, an object like a saint's dry and darkened finger-bone or the dusty threads of a burial shroud.

Like a relic, seeing it vivified my imagination and I felt connected across the chasm of time and space to the person who touched it and wore it. Relics allow you to be with those who are no longer here.

I saw Bowie in concert once, on his Reality Tour in the early 2000's. My seat in the amphitheater was about 100 yards away from the stage. I was never closer to the living Bowie than that, but at the exhibition, in a sense, I was only one foot away; close enough for him to see me too, if he was looking.

THE FANTASTIC VOYAGE (1997-2013-2016-20??)

Anonymous, Ireland

*N*OW WELL INTO THEIR autumnal years, it is an inescapable fact that those ageing pop stars that remain from the much feted mid-to-late twentieth century will soon vacate their temporal bodies. The grim realization that this fantastic voyage must inevitably turn to erosion hit home most strongly on Monday, January 11, 2016 when the world woke up to the gut-wrenching news that David Bowie had exited this earthly realm — if he was ever really grounded here at all — and had journeyed to another dimension. Put simply, Bowie's death prompted a public mourning that traversed the social boundaries of generation, nationality, creed, gender, class, and race.

When Bowie died I had been a fan for 19 years. I loved him. He was my companion. Not just a musical one. What Wordsworth says about the landscape is exactly what I want to say about Bowie: he was and is my anchor, my nurse, my guide, my heart, my soul, and my moral being. He meant and means everything to me.

The years I've chosen represent the first time I ever saw Bowie, and then two years in which I shared significant collective experiences with other fans via the internet. I am 'the internet age' fan and grateful for it because without the internet I would've been alone with my thoughts on the last two albums. In the 1990s, I had no one to share my views with. I liked "old man music," as one schoolmate so eloquently put it. Born in the year *Labyrinth* was released, I can only claim a vicarious and mediated experience of the perceived golden years of the 1970s. But I don't envy the older fans as I know the golden years for me were 1997, 2013 and 2016.

1997

1997 was my 1972. I was ten years old and was sitting on the floor in the kitchen watching the BBC favorite *Top of the Pops* just like generations of British and Irish kids before me had done when on came this motley crew of mis-shapes, mistakes, and misfits. Gail Ann Dorsey was wearing a tail and horns, Reeves Gabrels was looking resplendent in his leather trousers with a few feathers adorning his left shoulder, and David Bowie was looking like a devil to be quite frank — what with his red hair, an earring, a goatee, leather trousers and that tattered Union Jack frock coat. Only Zachary Alford looked normal. Just like a ten year old in 1972, I was perplexed at what I'd just seen and heard. And so I boarded the ship and embarked on my fantastic voyage. "Dead Man Walking" was my "Starman." *Buddha of Suburbia*, *Outside* and *Earthling* were my Berlin Trilogy.

What always strikes me is the parallels between my Bowie moment and the generation of British and Irish kids who pinpoint the seminal 1972 performance of "Starman" as their epiphany. The older fans always talk about how Bowie spoke to their feeling of otherness. I always felt a bit out of kilter in terms of being a shy child from a working class background who had an appetite for reading and a tendency to want to learn about and talk about highbrow concepts that were probably considered to be the province of the middle class and, hence, a little bit above my station. It was all there in his work and his interviews where he would routinely jump from existentialism, to Japanese folk art, to nostalgia for the future. In addition, his performance of characters initially to overcome shyness led me to Erving Goffman's 'presentation of the self' and George Herbert Mead's 'looking glass self' to apply to my own life albeit on a more low key level; I can't think of another artist who managed to straddle the highbrow and the popular with such aplomb. He was an intellectual and I will always admire the way in which he brought challenging ideas to a cultural form that has often been accused of being rather vacuous.

As previously stated, I was largely on my own in my love of Bowie until I got internet access albeit dial-up back in 2004. I signed up to Paul Kinder's *Bowie Wonderworld* (BWW) website and began chatting to other often older fans. The internet brought me into contact with some of the brightest and nicest people I have ever met. Here I was, a 'post-cold war kid', if you like, interacting with the 'children of the revolution' who had been there in the 1970s. The older fans never tried to wield their actual presence in the 1970s and 1980s as a form of power or extra knowledge. Instead, I was welcomed into the community with many of them delighted to see that Bowie's music was carrying on to another generation. Indeed, I felt I managed to transform my status from a 'passive observer from the Future' to an 'active participant in a lived fan culture' by interacting with the other fans online. I lived virtually through the video clips, images, stories and memories of the 1970s and 1980s which they so generously shared online. I even had the fortune to meet up with some of them in reality with one of them giving me a Bowie tour of London while another who visited Dublin left me some Australian jam and Tim Tams to pick up from the hotel in which she stayed. You can't beat Bowie fans for their warmth and thoughtfulness.

During these years, there wasn't the same level of action from Bowie that we had grown accustomed to but still I remember them very fondly precisely due to the internet and its creation of an amorphous non-time and non-space zone that brought together fans from all generations and corners of the globe. I laugh now at the memory of how we would get excited when a new paparazzi photo of him carrying his shopping would appear so barren were those years, and there were moments of genuine excitement arising from his performance in *The Prestige* and in *Extras*, for instance. During this time I was also busy working in a record shop and used my position to order every hard-to-find-turkey-of-a-film he had been in and played his records non-stop when the manager wasn't around. I once proudly played *Ziggy* six times in succession and managed to royally piss off the workers in the coffee shop and the book section.

In 2010 I began to doubt that Bowie would ever return and many of the old pals I used to chat to online had migrated to pastures anew though we all seemed to continue reading BWW. I distinctly remember sending a video to a friend in an email in Christmas 2012 of the most beautiful piano cover of 'Teenage Wildlife' (which a member had posted to BWW) while lamenting that we would probably never hear from him again. Little did I know there was something in the air...

2013

I remember it was a notably dark January morning, much darker than other mornings. I would generally glance at BWW for about five minutes max every morning. Still half asleep, I didn't even see the titles of the threads and just randomly clicked on one which contained the image of Bowie sitting under a photo of himself and Burroughs as he eyeballed the camera coolly. Bowie was back! And it was like an old friend calling to say 'hi'. Speaking of old friends, I reconnected with all my old Bowie pals online.

Though I had been a fan for many years, this was the first time I could share in a collective experience of a new Bowie album.

I grew up in a time without the large-scale original music youth cultures of the 1960s-1990s. Hence, the consumption of music had always been a largely solitary activity for me. If listening to new music in the bedroom with your mates represented a blood ritual for young people in the 20th century I would wager that chatting online to fellow fans represents something of a blood ritual in the 21st century. In 2013 with *The Next Day* and the internet I finally got my first taste of sharing a collective music experience and it was one of the best feelings ever.

2016

I was very excited about 2016 and was thinking to myself that Bowie might even tour again this year. We've got him back now like old times. He's going to make a record every 2-3 years. Normal service has resumed.

And so it was another exceptionally dark January morning. I got up even earlier than usual as I knew the roads would be icy so I would need extra time to get to my destination. I left my phone charging in my bedroom and went to the kitchen to have my breakfast. When I returned I noticed the blue light on my phone flashing and immediately had a bad feeling. It's like those phone calls in the middle of night when a loved one has passed away. My friends and family know better than to text me at 7.30am. This can't be good. But I never suspected what I was about to read. It was a text from a friend saying simply: "Oh no, Bowie has died!" I didn't initially panic because I thought my friend had simply got his wires crossed. I mean Bowie had just released a new album so surely that's what my friend meant. I logged onto my computer even though I knew this would delay me further and went onto BWW and there it was all confirmed. I went into shock and autopilot and just set off on my journey as I listened to my *Blackstar* CD. It really hadn't sunk in. I knew the tears were in the post but I had to be strong and act like nothing had happened. I just had to get safely to my destination and act normal until I could come home. It wasn't until later when I was coming home that I eventually had to pull over and let it all out. I was afraid I'd crash if I continued. I pulled in at the nearest spot which was beside a church and just cried and cried until I felt able to continue my journey home.

The contrast couldn't have been greater. We get him back. We don't get him back. We'll never get him back. Coincidentally I was already going through one of the worst periods of my life at this time. Once again, I found solace in the internet and re-connecting with old pals and, in some cases, people I hadn't spoken to online for seven years or more. I suspect we will come together every January hereafter to remember our man. These people are perhaps the biggest part of my Bowie story. Any time anything Bowie-related happened I would log on straight away to connect with them and share the excitement or, in this case, the sadness. The journey, however, has not just been about our connections between each other as fans but also the connection between the fans and Bowie online.

What strikes me is the connection Bowie had with the fans particularly with those last two albums. It really felt like he made those albums for us and since his death it has emerged that he did indeed keep an eye on what fans were saying online over the years. Twice on his birthday he gave us the gift. I just don't know any other artist like that. He had respect for us and for himself. He remained an innovator never becoming an excavator like his peers. Most of his contemporaries have become their own tribute acts going on nostalgia tour after nostalgia tour as they attempt to channel younger versions of themselves not to mention their acceptance of knighthoods and willing assimilation into the establishment. Bowie, on the other hand, was the real working class hero who never felt the need to scream from the rooftops about who he was and what he believed in. Empty vessels rattle the loudest. His quiet approach spoke volumes about his character and nature. He just kept doing exactly what he wanted to do. He kept pushing himself and us. To persevere and make the last album knowing that he likely wouldn't be around to enjoy its success is heartbreaking. I admire the quiet and unassuming way in which Bowie beavered away at his work and his commitment to art even in death.

As January looms I find myself thinking of him more and more again. I don't feel ashamed of feeling grief at his death. Bowie was big on the idea that his music was not a finished product until the audience got their hands on it and interpreted it. He posited this viewpoint on innumerable occasions in interviews over the years. Hence, I believe we met somewhere in the grey space in the middle within his music. We did know each other on some level.

I just hope he has found those English evergreens and as my throat tightens and my eyes inevitably well up again at the loss of one of my oldest companions I'll punctuate with a poignant farewell taken from a promotional clip he did for MTV for "Black Tie White Noise": "I hope to see you once again another day in another place." Bye-bye Spaceboy.

A BEAUTIFUL EXIT

Dara O'Kearney, Ireland

I WAS 18 YEARS OLD when I became a lifelong David Bowie fan. That summer, I did my leaving cert, and was counting down the days til I left my parents' home. I saw it as an escape from a deeply unhappy household and childhood. It seemed like from the moment I could understand what she was saying, my mother wanted to re-enforce that life was a pile of shit, all attempts to succeed at anything or find love with anyone were doomed to fail, and it was best not to even try. Growing up in small town Ireland at the time with the widely held views that any sort of ambition was just getting notions above your station simply added to the unhappiness. So it's fair to say as I left with my mother's words of "You'll never amount to anything" ringing in my ears, I was in the market for other parental role models with more appealing messages. David Bowie, a seemingly reluctant star who critiqued and criticized his own fame, with his central message for outsiders (that no matter how much of an outsider or loser or weirdo you feel like at times, you do not have to conform to the restrictions and demands of others, and the only person you really have to answer to is yourself) seemed ideal. Most of the other fans I talked to after his death expressed surprise and even dismay at the depth of feeling his passing had engendered in them (Bowie

271

fans tend to be cynics by nature; one even lamented, "Good God, I feel like all those pathetic Princess Diana people.") The reason for this, I think, was Bowie was the guy who reached fans who never wanted to be "fans" of anyone in the first place. An icon for iconoclasts, an idol for people who were uncomfortable at the very notion of idolatry: this was Bowie's hardcore appeal. His unparalleled individualism attracted individuals who are naturally uncomfortable at any sort of supposed communal experience. He appealed to non-conformists, oddities and outsiders.

Over the next ten years, Bowie was undoubtedly the biggest single influence on my thinking on practically everything. I avidly devoured all his interviews, everything written on him. By the mid-90s when the Internet started to be a thing, and most people started to think it could be a thing for porn or gambling, my first reaction was it could be a thing to share my passion for all things Bowie with other Bowie freaks. For roughly five years, my main pastime was my involvement in the online Bowie fan world that revolved around a Usenet group, a few fan websites, and a couple of mailing lists. The knowledge I had absorbed from ten years of obsessively reading everything related to Bowie meant I acquired a depth of superficial "knowledge" (from a purely fan perspective) that few others had. To my surprise, this meant other fans from all around the world started asking me questions and I was seen as something of an authority. I wrote reviews, fan articles, lengthy posts. Much of my social life revolved around my interactions with Bowie fans.

Bowie himself was something of an Internet pioneer. He quickly saw what it was going to become at a time when people like Jeremy Paxman protested "but it's just another method of distribution." There were rumours backed up by pretty solid indicators that Bowie spent a lot of time reading what his fans said and wrote about him. This was consistent with his stated self-declaration that he was an artist who believed that the art was not complete until the audience had added its piece (he saw art not as something that ended when the artist delivered a piece but rather only started at that point, and was completed by the interpretations of the audience). This added an interesting dynamic to the Bowie online fan world, given that fans often believed their posts were read by the artist himself. One consequence of this was the rise of the impersonators: fans who got their jollies by pretending to be Bowie (or someone close to him, or even just other fans: I had a few impersonators of my own). The more transparent ones openly claimed it; the smarter ones just hinted at it enigmatically. Some were convincing enough to the point that some fans (myself included) believed it was possible it really was Bowie. At least one almost certainly, actually was.

Sometime in the late 90s, I started getting emails from someone I initially believed to be a very clever impersonator from the "enigmatic hints" camp. This person expressed themselves in a manner becoming of someone of Bowie's erudition, was well researched (no obvious factual errors), and never posted at a time when Bowie clearly couldn't have. They never stated themselves to be Bowie but clearly spoke from his perspective, and the emails were always signed simply "db." All the emails were coming from an email address that started with the letters "bxqr": when I suggested to my correspondent suspiciously that those letters brought the words "Bowie, Ex Queer" to my mind, my correspondent simply responded "Mine too, but sadly not before I chose four seemingly random letters." I decided to keep an open mind that it might.. might..be Bowie. Even if it wasn't, the person was funny enough and interesting enough in themselves to be worth spending time corresponding with. The correspondence grew over time from a few short snappy emails a week to sometimes three or four quite long and in depth discussions a day. This initially left me less inclined to believe I really was corresponding with Bowie himself; after all, he really should have better things to be doing with his time than swapping emails with a fan, right? I kept trying to catch him out; either on facts, or with tricks like emailing him just as I knew he was going on stage in New York or wherever, hoping the impersonator would answer instantly thereby removing all doubt. I never caught him out. I ran searches on the email address to see what popped up (trolls who like to impersonate celebrities are generally not smart enough to use different email addresses). Nothing did. I decided to ask a friend who worked with him musically a favor: I asked him to confirm or deny that the email address was the same one Bowie used to correspond with him. My friend was understandably wary, given how guarded Bowie was about his privacy. In the end, we agreed on just four letters and he confirmed that yes, the email address he dealt with also started with "bxqr." At this point I decided that yes, it was David Bowie I was corresponding with, at least some of the time.

In late 2003, Bowie came to Dublin to perform two concerts at the Point Theatre. They were filmed for a concert video, which would turn out to be his last ever. I had made it a rule from the start that I would never ask my correspondent for a favour that Bowie could grant (even though this could have quickly cleared up whether it was really him or not). My other rule was I would never reveal to anyone anything he told me in confidence, something which goes against my natural blabbermouth tendencies and something he remarked on favourably a few times conspiratorially ("I probably shouldn't be telling you this, but I haven't seen you spill anything I told you before, so...") Tickets were tough to come by but by now I was an old hand with a good network, so I secured two tickets for both nights which sold out in minutes. My correspondent sent a message saying, "I hear both concerts sold out instantly so I've put you plus one on the guest list." I withheld the information that I already had two tickets: this seemed like the chance to prove (or disprove) the notion that I was dealing with Bowie, and even if I was the victim of a ridiculously elaborate hoax and this was supposed to be the payoff (humiliation trying to get into a concert claiming to be on the guest list), well, I still had my two purchased tickets as backup.

In the run up to the concert, I was inundated by messages from fans desperate to get their hands on tickets. I initially just sympathized with their plight, but then started to feel bad at the thought that I might be able to get in without my tickets and then they would go unused. So I relented and told one guy who waxed at length how he had never seen Bowie live and feared he never would (there were already rumours this would be Bowie's last ever tour) and how it would be life changing for him and his boyfriend to see him in concert, that I might...might...be able to help. I arranged to meet him in town before the concert, at a nearby pub, planning to shoot off at some point to find out if I was actually on the guest list, and return with the tickets if I was.

So about an hour before the concert, I present myself to the security representative, mumbling that I think I might..might..be on some sort of a guest list. The security man in question, a real salt of the earth built like a shit brickhouse type with an accent that strongly suggested at a life spent mostly in Tallaght, looked at me suspiciously.

"You might...might be on a guest list bud? What makes you think that?"

I mumbled very unsurely that I had been told I was.

"I didn't even know there was a guest list."

I mumbled something that may have been "Oh, I see."

The security representative shouted, "Bill! Bill! Is there a guest list for tonight?"

I now found myself looking at an even bigger security man, also more than likely from Tallaght.

"Who wants to know, Ben?"

"This gentleman thinks there might be..and he might... might...be on it."

Bill looked at me suspiciously.

"What's your name, pal?"

Showing admirable powers of recollection in the face of such pressure, I somehow managed to remember my own name.

Ben pulled out a one page list that looked like it had at most two lines printed on it. He looked at one of the lines, looked at me.

"Yeah pal, your name is here, plus one. Where's your plus one?"

With that, I scooted off to the pub to collect plus one and give the two lads the spare tickets.

Earlier that day, I had swapped emails with my correspondent as we watched the rugby World Cup final between England and Australia. For those who don't remember, it was a thrillingly close encounter. In the last minute of the match, Australia kicked a penalty to level the match and send it to extra time. Two minutes into extra time, England kicked a penalty to take the lead, which they held until three minutes from the end, when an Australian penalty again leveled the scores. With 26 seconds remaining on the clock, Wilkinson scored a drop kick to win the World Cup for England.

As a patriotic Englishman, my correspondent was understandably delighted. He asked if he should mention the match on stage that evening, if Irish fans would be likely to share his delight. I suggested it might be wiser not to, not just because we have a long history of cheering for anyone *but* England, but also because I didn't feel many rugby fans were Bowie fans, and vice versa. I jokingly suggested if it was crowd pleasing banter he wanted, *Tiocfaidh Ar La* might do the job better (for those who don't know, this is a rather mischievous idea given that it was the IRA slogan at the time.) He asked me for the phonetic pronunciation and I played along.

To my surprise, Bowie opened the concert with those three words.

That tour would prove to be his final one. It was curtailed

the following year when he suffered a heart attack and was subsequently diagnosed with an acutely blocked artery that required an angioplasty procedure.

After his recovery, Bowie seemed to move into retirement comfortably and devote himself to be a full time Dad to his young daughter, Lexi. There were intermittent cameos, but no more albums, and the retirement seemed permanent. Our correspondence tapered off and I was forced to find other pastimes. My running career took off unexpectedly when what was intended as a farewell appearance in the New York ultra marathon in Central Park ended in improbably victory. Earlier today, I went back though my old emails and found that incredibly in the week before I flew to New York, Bowie sent me some useful links on things to see and do in New York, and immediately after the race, he was one of the first to congratulate me. As my poker career took off, he feigned some interest or at least amusement at my latest improbable career twist. I joke that it was his fault; without any new Bowie albums to obsess over, I had to find some other outlet for my compulsions. This was intended as a joke, but like many jokes has more than a grain of truth. I actually did need to find another hobby to replace reading Bowie interviews. Without Bowie's influence on my mindset and his view that even if everything is not possible you should at least give it your all before giving up, I would not have been the sort of 42 year old who knew nothing about poker but would still look at an online poker landscape dominated by guys younger than my kids and think, "Hey, maybe I could do that."

As poker took over my life, and with Bowie in apparent retirement, my social life no longer revolved around the Bowie fan world, any correspondence with the man himself withered to a few messages a year, usually around birthdays or holidays. I guess the sad reality was that I wasn't really all that interested in the latest episode of SpongeBob (a firm doting Daddy/daughter favorite it seems) and he had no interest in hearing my latest bad beat stories.

In the early hours of the 8th of January, 2013 (Bowie's 66th birthday), I was winding down my nightly online session on a final table, when I opened Twitter to find it had exploded with news that at midnight Bowie had released his first new single in almost a decade, with no pre-publicity or fanfare. He'd simply put the new song up at his website, and the world went crazy. Within hours, "Where Are We Now?" had topped the iTunes charts. As I signed on to Gmail to send him a "Happy Birthday but WTF?" message, I saw an email from an old familiar address that had sat unopened for days (I no longer check my email daily) that simply said "Something is coming."

That summer, I travelled back from Las Vegas with Daragh Davey at the end of the World Series of Poker. We had a few hours to kill in London en route, so I dragged Daragh into central London to the "David Bowie Is..." exhibition. As a general rule I like to keep my obsessions and my compulsions separate. I try not to bore runners and Bowie fans with bad beat stories, and I generally no more than hint at a previous life as a hardcore Bowie fan (much less a correspondent) to my poker buddies. So Daragh had no real idea why we were even going to such a thing.

He seemed suitably impressed though, and as I scanned the gift shop afterwards for merchandise I didn't already own, he thumbed through one of the many Bowie biographies, before his eyes widened and he exclaimed, "Oh my God! You're mentioned in here!" It takes a lot to get young Daragh excited to the point of exclamation about anything, so that's right up there as one of my favourite moments in poker.

My emails with David remained intermittent the last few years. When I wrote what many people think is my best ever blog about my son Oisin, I thought of David a lot and the advice he occasionally offered as one father to another. I ended that blog with a Philip Larkin poem which Bowie had told me was his favourite, on the difficulties of parenthood (one thing we shared was we were both products of unhappy homes with ill-suited parents.) Over the next couple of days I agonized over whether it was even advisable to even publish a blog that had no relation to poker, so I sent it first to some close poker friends and to David. This is another such blog, but one I sadly can't send him for his thumbs up or down.

In the early hours of January 10, 2016, I was winding down after a long Sunday grind watching bad TV, when I chanced onto an RTE News segment waxing lyrical about Bowie's acclaimed latest album, *Blackstar*. I drifted off to sleep happily thinking about the beautiful new album, not yet realizing it was a beautiful farewell note, and remembering that I hadn't sent my customary Happy Birthday email. It can wait till morning, I thought.

I woke up to a message from Sean, one of the many great friends I gained through Bowie saying he felt absurd and mortified to be thinking this way, but he felt like he'd lost a close friend of 40 years. Like most hardcore Bowie fans, Sean is a hardened cynic by nature, and also has never allowed his fandom to obscure his ability to criticize and critique Bowie and his work when he felt it came up short. So I initially thought "Oh...he doesn't like the new album, and he's being overly dramatic." But then it suddenly hit me...it might...might..and with a sinking heart I signed on to Twitter and saw Bowie was trending ahead of Justin Bieber by several million tweets. It couldn't just be reaction to the new album.

I spent the rest of the day feeling as sad and grief stricken as I ever have in my life, while simultaneously sharing Sean's mortification and sense of absurdity that I felt like this in a world where millions of Syrians are starving, over a celebrity I never even had a face to face conversation with. I still can't really explain it, other than to say Bowie was the single biggest influence on my life and how I have chosen to live it. He was an idol and an icon to people like me who scoff at such notions, he was the closest thing to a father figure I've had in my life, he was a thrillingly sharp, bright and funny correspondent for several years, and he helped me with things as small as the best website for what's happening in New York to things as big as to how you should think about and live life on your own terms. It was never a relationship of anything even approaching equals yet he never lorded his exalted status over me (he was polite and solicitous to a fault). I got an insight into the sharpest mind I've ever encountered; at worst all he got from me was pathetic devotion and at best perhaps a few interesting questions at times and the correct pronunciation of *Tiocfaidh ar la*.

Early in his life, Bowie mastered the perfect dramatic entrance, and he left us with the most graceful of exits. He leaves a beautiful farewell album and a touching final video, one I feel certain will go down as one of the most artful exists in history. All I have is this dreadfully inadequate blog which doesn't even scratch the surface of what this genius meant to millions of fans like me, or start to explain just how and why he meant to much to all of us. I can find no words other than goodbye David, it was a privilege to know you even a little.

CONTRIBUTORS

Anonymous, UK
Anonymous, Ireland
Bella Aptekar
Sandra (Spidey) Atkins
Patrick Bamburak
Theresa Bradley
Patti Brett
Artemis Burns
Chris Buxbaum
Gwenn Catterfeld
Tracy Chorlton
Stuart Dalzell
John Davey
Ruth Davison
Jean Marie Dawson
Mark W. Falzini
Isabelle Flows
Mike Gately
Sheva Golkow
Denise Heptinstall
Chris Hughes
Eric Isaacson
Peter Jackson
Kali and Belle

Marla Kanevsky
Paul Kinder
Kathryn Kopple
Melanie Krichel
Dorothy Kulisek
Daniel F. LeRay
Alyson Lewis
Steve Lock
Randy Marthins
Simone Metge
Linda Metz
Jackie Miles
Frank Moriarty
Ray Nash
Petter M. Ness
Billy Nevins
Wendy Norman
Dara O'Kearney
Debbie Pagel
Alyssa Linn Palmer
Patrizia Pezzola
Christina Prass
Princess Ramsey
Will Putney
Johnny Quest
RaMoana
Charlie Raven
Sam
Jenn Staib
Julie Stoller
Jasmine Storm
Barbara Streun
Lisa Taylor

Caroline Thompson
Kevin White
Bob Wigo
Dave Wisniewski

READER RESOURCES

$\mathcal{T}$HE FOLLOWING IS NOT intended to be a complete listing of all David Bowie recordings and websites but only those referenced within this book. The list is provided for clarification purposes and the reader's ability to more easily research and locate these recordings and sites if they chose.

Select Discography

Space Oddity
November 4, 1969
Philips, Mercury

The Man Who Sold the World
November 4, 1970
Mercury

Hunky Dory
December 17, 1971
RCA

The Rise and Fall of Ziggy Stardust and the Spiders from Mars
June 6, 1972
RCA

Aladdin Sane
April 13, 1973
RCA

Pin Ups
October 19, 1973
RCA

Diamond Dogs
May 24, 1974
RCA

Young Americans
March 7, 1975
RCA

Station to Station
January 23, 1976
RCA

Low
January 14, 1977
RCA

Heroes
October 14, 1977
RCA

Lodger
May 18, 1979
RCA

Scary Monsters (And Super Creeps)
September 12, 1980
RCA

Let's Dance
April 14, 1983
EMI

Tonight
September 1, 1984
EMI

Never Let Me Down
April 27, 1987
EMI

Tin Machine
May 22, 1989
EMI

Tin Machine II
September 2, 1991
London

Black Tie White Noise
April 5, 1993
Arista, BMG

Outside
September 26, 1995
RCA

Earthling
February 3, 1997
RCA

Hours
October 4, 1999
Virgin

Bowie at the Beeb
September 26, 2000
EMI

Heathen
June 11, 2002
ISO/Columbia

Reality
September 16, 2003
ISO/Columbia

The Next Day
March 8, 2013
ISO/Columbia

Blackstar
January 8, 2016
ISO/Columbia

Websites:

Teenage Wildlife (teenagewildlife.com)
BowieNet (davidbowie.com)
Bowie Wonderworld (bowiewonderworld.com)

"Knowledge comes with death's release"

David Bowie

"Quicksand" *Hunky Dory* 1971

Printed in the United States
By Bookmasters